Contemporary Issues
A Christian View

James and Audrey Bentley

Audrey W Bentley began her teaching career in a boys' public school. She subsequently taught in junior schools and in a 'special' school for difficult children. Today she is deputy head of the Brigidine Convent School in Windsor, having been senior mistress at the Church of England High School, Eccles.

Her qualifications include a certificate of education from the University of Leeds, and an M.Ed. for a thesis on nineteenth-century religious education in a Lancashire mill town.

James Bentley has taught religion in junior and secondary schools, and to mature students at Liverpool University, and at Eton College (where he was senior chaplain). He has also been Maurice Reckitt research fellow in Christian social thought at the University of Sussex.

He holds Oxford degrees in Modern History and Theology, an Oxford B.D., and a D. Phil. of the University of Sussex. His books include a life of Pastor Niemöller and *A Calendar of Saints.*

Contents

Introduction

Christians, like everyone else, disagree about the answers to many of the major social issues of our time. Take the 53 million North American Catholics, for instance. Almost half of them are regular church-goers (compared with an average of 15 per cent in Europe). Yet when it comes to such an important question as whether women subjected to rape should be allowed abortions, even though the Catholic Church is officially totally opposed to abortion, nearly 69 per cent of these American Catholics say yes.

On another personal issue, whether or not divorce is ever acceptable to Christians, only one-third of Roman Catholics in the USA support the church in saying no.

Clearly, American Christians like to make up their own minds. So do non-Catholics, Protestants, Anglicans and members of the great churches of the East. So do unbelievers and those of other faiths.

This book aims to help us do the same. We want the students who use it to work out their own personal responses to key issues. To do this does not mean neglecting the great resources available to us in the Christian tradition:

the Bible above all, a remarkable treasure of moral insight;
the decrees of councils and popes;
the thinking of such international Christian bodies as the World Council of Churches;
the contribution of Quakers and pacifists;
the example and teaching of many devoted Christian men and women of today and the past.

Religious and non-religious beliefs deeply influence our world, and we explore in our book the way they do so. Also, while chiefly exploring the profound social teachings of the Jewish-Christian tradition, we look occasionally at other great world religions besides Christianity.

Since no sound decision on how to live can be made without carefully looking at all the factual aspects of the difficult problems our world faces, this book offers much background material as well as the sources for finding out more.

We also strongly urge students to make up their own brochures on these different issues — folders made up of newspaper cuttings, magazine articles, information gathered from such groups as War on Want or Help the Aged. In that way each student will become increasingly conversant with what is happening in our world.

Of course, this book does not have space to deal with every urgent social issue of today. For example, we do not discuss male homosexuality and lesbianism, AIDS, or the alternatives people have suggested to the traditional Christian family. We are also conscious that some aspects of present-day society have only been mentioned, without being discussed in depth. One such aspect is the deep-rooted effects of colonialism on British society and on traditional British attitudes to other nations and races. But no single book can deal with every contemporary social issue.

Great social issues are never easy to solve but our world is by no means all gloom. There are signs of hope even amidst the most daunting problems. Human beings have the capacity for happiness. Out book is intended as a contribution towards making the world a happier, more joyful, more compassionate place.

Audrey W Bentley
James Bentley

1 Racial Prejudice and Discrimination

Jesus's teaching — Jews and Christians

The good Samaritan

In Jesus's time two groups of people, Samaritans and Jews, could scarcely tolerate each other. In theory this should never have happened, for both Jews and Samaritans shared the same Holy Books from which they drew their rules of life. One of these rules was quite clear about how to treat strangers: exactly as you treat yourself. The reason for this was the Bible's belief that God has made everyone. Both strangers and your own people belong equally to him. As you are, the Bible says, so shall the stranger be in the eyes of God. (Numbers chapter 15, verses 15f) Yet a hundred years before the birth of Jesus some Jews had even burned down the Samaritans' holiest building, their Temple.

As a Jew, Jesus might have been expected to share his fellow Jews' dislike of Samaritans. Instead he tried always to bring about peace between the two groups.

He ordered his followers to love their neighbours as they loved themselves. Once he was asked, 'Who is my neighbour?' His reply was to tell a story about a good Samaritan and a stranger in trouble. Two other characters appear in the story: a priest and a Levite, who were supposed to set a good example to their fellow Jews. In this story they don't.

> A man was going down from Jerusalem to Jericho, and he fell among robbers, who stripped him, beat him and then left him half dead.
>
> Now by chance a priest was going down that road; and when he saw him he passed by on the other side. In the same way a Levite, when he came to the place and saw him, passed by on the other side. But a Samaritan, as he

journeyed, came to where he was; and when he saw him, he had compassion, and went up to him and bound up his wounds, pouring on oil and wine. Then he set him on his own beast and brought him to an inn, and took care of him. The next day he took out two days' wages and gave them to the innkeeper. 'Take care of the man,' he said, 'and if you spend anything more, I will repay you when I come back.'

Jesus turned to the man who had asked 'Who is my neighbour?' and now asked him, which of the three who had come across the man in trouble turned out to be a good neighbour. The man replied, 'The one who showed mercy on him.' Jesus said to him, 'Go and do the same.' (Luke chapter 10, verses 30 to 37, Revised Standard Version)

Plainly Jesus is saying two things: that strangers needing our care must be helped; and that the Samaritans, a group very much disliked by his own people, included fine people. Yet despite this clear teaching and command, Christians have not always treated strangers with kindness. They are not alone in this kind of behaviour.

1 Reasons for hostility towards strangers

Fear

One reason for failing to treat strangers decently is simply that many people tend to fear (or at least distrust) new faces. A cartoon in *Punch* once showed two city boys watching a stranger coming down the street. 'Who's that?' asked one. 'Don't know,' replied the other. 'Then heave half a brick at him,' said the first.

Secondly, the more differences there are between groups of people, the harder it is for them to understand and come to terms with each other. In theory the fact that, for instance, different groups of people do not share the same religion is no reason at all for them hating each other. But in the Middle Ages Christians would force Jews to live in separate parts of the towns and cities, whether the Jews liked this or not.

Ghettoes

These areas were known as 'ghettoes'. Jews were forbidden to marry Christians.

2 Cruelty to Jews

Black Death

In times of national disaster, cruelty to Jews grew much worse. When the Black Death brought terror to the whole of Europe in 1348, since nobody knew that a kind of black rat brought the plague, many people decided that the Jews were poisoning wells to kill Christians.

Even though Pope Clement VI, the leader of Western Christians at this time, issued a stern letter declaring that this accusation against Jews was a lie, his Christian followers mostly disregarded it. Whole Jewish families were dragged from their houses and thrown on to bonfires or murdered in equally hideous ways. To give just one example, in 1349 the citizens of Basle in Switzerland constructed a huge wooden house on an island in the River Rhine, shut inside it the whole Jewish population of the city — hundreds of them — and set them all alight.

Irrational behaviour

This behaviour, as well as being utterly savage, was also absurd. As Pope Clement had pointed out, the Black Death was killing Jews as well as Christians. Why should Jews want to poison themselves? He also argued that since the Black Death was as rife in towns and cities where there were no Jews as elsewhere, the Jews quite simply could not be to blame.

His arguments, though correct, made no difference. This indicates an extremely important fact about such behaviour: that it is not based on reason.

Prejudice

The word we usually use to describe this unthinking hatred is 'prejudice'. A prejudiced person feels threatened by any other group than the one he or she belongs to. Sometimes the other group may be richer or more powerful. Many Jews in the Middle Ages made their living as money-lenders (it was often the only job they were allowed to do), and those obliged to borrow off them resented them. This is one reason why prejudice against the Jews developed into deep hatred.

Resentment

If the 'outsiders' seem weaker, then the prejudiced persons often try to dominate them. So Jesus's command, 'Love your neighbour as yourself' is ignored. Instead the outsider is treated with hostility and aggression. Alarming figures produced in 1986 by the Runnymede Trust indicate that some white people in Britain are treating our black (i.e. ethnic minority) population in precisely this way. In Britain whites attack the homes or persons of blacks on average once every 26 minutes.

'Threat' of the 'outsider'

Why are prejudiced people 'threatened' by those who *seem* actually weaker than themselves? Of course a threat from another person may well be real. For instance, if someone breaks into your home, the sooner you get police help the better. To dislike burglars is not a 'prejudice'. But to feel threatened by whole groups of people just because they are 'outsiders' and differ in some ways from your own group is quite another matter. It means that you are refusing to see each member of the other group as an individual person, capable of being loved and hurt, capable of giving love or hurting, with hopes and fears and ambitions and needs just like your own. It means that every member of the other group seems threatening or inferior.

1 Racists

Racists believe that some groups of people are naturally inferior to their own group. They believe there are factual reasons for accepting this.

Assertion of superiority

In the past two hundred years it has usually been the richest and the dominant nations that have had the arrogance to decide that *they* are the superior people. The European whites have been particularly prone to this. In response some black people (such as the Black Muslim groups) have asserted their own superiority over whites.

No one, of course, ever asserts their own inferiority! And all these racists fail to produce the remotest scientific evidence for their own claims to belong to the best race in the world.

2 Racial prejudice

Colour prejudice

The special danger of racial prejudice as opposed to other kinds of prejudice is that the groups regarded as inferior can sometimes be very clearly distinguished by the colour of their skin. People may therefore avoid even trying to meet members of the group they dislike. A black person applying for a job, may simply not be offered an interview (if their colour is known in advance); or, when they come for the interview, they may not be taken seriously.

When two consultants at the medical school of St George's Hospital, South London, looked into the way the school selected medical students, they discovered that (consciously or unconsciously) selection was extremely biased first against women and then, much more, against non-whites. If you were a woman, your chances of being interviewed went down by three points; if you were non-white your chances of an interview were up to 20 points lower!

3 The Race Relations Act

Against the law

Now not only are all these attitudes contrary to the teachings of the Bible and the teachings of Jesus; they are also against Britain's Race Relations Act, passed in 1976. As a result of this act, the victims of prejudice can sometimes fight back. For instance, in December 1986 three British Asians working for British Telecom complained to an industrial tribunal of the way they had been abused by a senior member of British Telecom's staff. The industrial tribunal awarded the three men a total of £1,500. In addition British Telecom was ordered to 'ensure that all supervisory staff at all levels are fully aware of the provisions of the Race Relations Act'.

Discrimination

Discrimination occurs when either the habits or the laws of a society start to deny to certain groups their normal rights.

Racial discrimination in employment

'Discrimination' is thus a further, severe consequence of prejudice, particularly racial prejudice. Few experts in Britain today think we have much discrimination written into our laws. This does not mean that we do not see here a lot of conscious or unconscious discrimination and prejudice. It has been estimated that 30 per cent of British firms discriminate (either consciously or unconsciously) against black people in their employment policies.

Disadvantages

Discrimination can be made worse simply by the disadvantages of a new immigrant group. Take as an example the Bangladeshis, the most recent group of immigrants to Britain from Asia.

They amount to no more than 100,000 people. Coming from the rural Sylhet region of north-west Bangladesh, many of them have experienced great difficulties coping with industrial Britain, especially as most of them now live in our major cities. Also, nearly three-quarters of them by the age of 15 are not fluent in English. Finally, many of them have only been able to find accommodation in areas where the deteriorating housing stock is badly in need of new building.

Unable to speak English well, many of them find it difficult to make good use of our social services and our health service. Not surprisingly, the average wage of British Bangladeshis is smaller than that of any other group in the country; their unemployment rate is higher; the houses they live in include the worst and the most overcrowded in the country.

Poor conditions

Alongside this kind of discrimination, our own century has also seen two of the most determined and savage exercises in racial discrimination.

Adolf Hitler

The most savage discrimination occurred in Germany between 1933 and 1945, under the sway of its chancellor, Adolf Hitler. All his life Hitler had hated Jews, and to a lesser extent (but still viciously) Gypsies and black people. Hitler's remarks about these people hardly bear repeating. For instance, forbidding marriage between what he called 'pure' Germans and other races, he wrote that the children of such marriages would be 'monstrosities halfway between man and ape'.

Preserving the 'pure' German

As early as 1919, long before he became the dictator of Germany, Adolf Hitler had written that all Jews should be forcibly removed from Germany. (He did not say where they should be sent.) Jews had been thrown out of many countries in Christian Europe — including England, France, Portugal and Spain — at various periods throughout the centuries.

Suggesting that groups of people had no place in their own country soon led on to much more vicious behaviour. Hitler next formed a political party: the National Socialists, or 'Nazis'. Its programme, set out in 1920, declared that no Jew would be allowed to remain a member of the German nation. If the Nazis came to power, the programme stated, any Jew who had arrived in Germany since 1914 would be expelled.

The Nazi party

In 1924, while he was in prison for trying to overthrow the German republic, Hitler wrote a book (named *Mein Kampf*, meaning 'My Struggle') which attacked Jews with wild and horrible accusations. 'Black-haired Jewish youths lie in wait

'Mein Kampf'

for hours, glaring like Satan at unsuspicious girls, spying on them, planning to seduce them, adulterating their blood,' he wrote.

His remarks today seem those of a maniac; and he combined his hatred of Jews with his hatred of blacks. He declared: 'The Jews were responsible for bringing negroes into the land, with the final aim of bastardising the white race which they hate and plan to rule.'

Hitler gave all Jews evil characters out of his own diseased imagination. Many people in Germany who voted for Hitler's party in the general election had probably never even read Hitler's *Mein Kampf*, but shared Hitler's irrational hatred of the Jews and displayed typical racism in refusing to see them as individuals.

Hitler set up gangs of thugs, dressed in uniform and known as 'Brownshirts', to terrorise and even beat up those who disagreed with his views. The tactics of the Nazis were crude but unfortunately effective. In the elections held in

The glasses of murdered prisoners in a Nazi concentration camp

October 1931, Hitler's party gained six million votes and thus became the second largest in the German parliament.

By 1933 Hitler was Germany's leading politician, its chancellor. In that year another 33 German Jews had been murdered and countless others brutally beaten up by his followers. Soon Jews were being sent to special 'concentration camps'. Their places of worship (synagogues) were smashed and set on fire. They were thrown out of their jobs, and forbidden to take up any work paid for by the state (such as, for instance, teaching).

Concentration camps

Worse was to follow. Hitler was determined to expand Germany, and by 1939 he was at war, his opponents including the British. At first he was tremendously successful, conquering Poland, Czechoslovakia, Norway, Holland, Belgium and France with ease.

Wherever Hitler's armies went, his followers began to persecute the Jews. Finally the Germans put in operation what was known as the 'final solution' to the problem of the Jews: their total extermination. (This 'final solution' also applied to Gypsies.) When Hitler came to power there were around 490,000 German Jews. Very few of these survived. And by the time Hitler's armies were defeated and he himself had committed suicide in 1945, six million Jews throughout his domains had been mercilessly massacred.

The 'final solution'

Apartheid

Attempts such as Hitler's to destroy whole races are the most vicious form of racism. The name for this kind of murderous racism is 'genocide'. Another form is known as 'apartheid'.

Apartheid is a system developed by South Africans who emigrated to that country from Holland and are known as Afrikaners. As well as English, they speak a form of Dutch known as Afrikaans, and *apartheid* is the Afrikaans word for 'apartness' or 'separation'.

Meaning of apartheid

The whites are in a minority in South Africa, and those of Dutch descent form around 60 per cent of them. The aim of those who support apartheid is to divide South Africa into separate regions for the whites and the blacks, and for the white minority to dominate the black majority.

The history of apartheid

The first Dutch settlers in South Africa three hundred years ago met only a yellow-skinned people, the Khoi Khoi, whom they called Hottentots, and another group they called Bushmen. No blacks lived where the Dutch initially settled, becoming wandering farmers ('Boers' in Afrikaans), with coloured people as their slaves.

The British take over

In 1815 the Dutch sold their colony to Britain for £6 million. The settlers were aghast to find that the British first insisted that they educate their slaves and then demanded that they set them free. Half of the Dutch set off on a great trek north to escape British rule. In new lands they created communities which always restricted to the white-skinned the right of voting and becoming a full citizen.

Gold and diamonds

In 1867 huge diamond deposits were found at Kimberley in South Africa. Nineteen years later, in 1886, the largest gold deposits in the world were discovered near Johannesburg. The British decided to take over the lands of the trekkers. The leader of the Afrikaners, a man named Paul Kruger, thought otherwise. He trapped the private army of a Britisher named Leander Jameson, who had attempted to overthrow him.

In 1899 the British went to war against the Afrikaners. This 'Boer War' was eventually won only after the British troops had behaved with total brutality. For instance, they herded children, women and old people into concentration camps, where 26,000 of them died. The British, however, could not run South Africa without the help of the Afrikaners they had defeated. In 1910 they gave the colony self-government. But — a crucial decision — they gave no power to the blacks. The whites were totally in control. Only a few blacks in Cape Province had the right to vote.

The African National Congress

Three years after the British handed over power a number of blacks, most of them educated by the Christian missionaries, founded the African National Congress. Their aim was to persuade the world outside that the blacks had rights and to campaign inside South Africa for those rights. Their activities petered out. In 1936 even those blacks who once had the right to vote in Cape Province had that right taken away.

The whites' problems were not over. Mining gold and diamonds is dangerous and hard. Blacks preferred to work on their own farms. So the whites passed an act barring blacks from owning, buying or living on 93 per cent of South Africa. The blacks were confined to their 'reserves'. But many of the white Afrikaners were also poor, especially after the price of gold fell in the 1920s. Their political leaders were determined that the poor whites should not be worse off than the blacks.

Black 'reserves'

During the war against Adolf Hitler, South Africa supported Britain. Many blacks were given new freedoms because of the need to employ them in armaments factories and in making army uniforms. The Afrikaners grew anxious that their own privileged position would soon be lost. After the war their leader, Dr Daniel François Malan, fought the 1948 election with the promise to get rid of what he called the 'black peril'. His party won the election, and he introduced the system of apartheid.

The 'black peril'

Verwoerd's measures

Dr Malan appointed as his minister in charge of Black Affairs a man named H F Verwoerd who had been a student in Germany during the Hitler years and welcomed Nazi racist ideas. He had blacks forcibly removed from the towns. He stopped blacks learning English in their schools, in spite of the protests of Christian missionaries who ran many of these schools. Although some white South Africans protested that the tiny 13 per cent of the country reserved for blacks was far too small and impoverished to support them, Verwoerd paid no attention. In 1958 he became prime minister of South Africa.

His plan now was to deprive blacks of any claim to be South African citizens by suggesting that their own reserves (or 'homelands') should be regarded as independent states. Chief Matanzima of one homeland, Transkei, accepted the plan. Its citizens immediately lost all their rights in white South Africa.

The influential black leader, Chief Gatsha Buthelezi (whose Zulu people outnumber all South African whites), rejected the whole plan. Blacks, he insisted, were citizens of South Africa, even if they also possessed their own homelands.

The ANC again

In 1955 the African National Congress organised a rally of 3,000 members, who set up a Freedom Charter, insisting that 'No government can justly claim authority unless it is based on the will of the people'. The South African government responded by arresting 156 of the leaders of the African National Congress, on the grounds that they were committing treason against the state.

Their trial lasted five years. It made famous a black

Violent confrontation between black and white: South African police attacking demonstrators

Nelson Mandela

defence lawyer, Nelson Mandela, who had joined the African National Congress in 1942 and was himself arrested. In 1960 Mandela was acquitted of treason. But in that year, when a peaceful crowd of 5,000 blacks assembled to demand their natural rights at a township called Sharpeville, police opened fire and killed 69 of them, wounding another 180. Most had been shot in the back.

Nelson Mandela now believed that only by violence would the South African system be compelled to change. He became the leader of a campaign to sabotage vital factories but to avoid targeting people. The African National Congress was banned. The government introduced a system under which men and women could be jailed without trial. In 1962 Nelson Mandela was arrested and sentenced to life imprisonment. He has remained in prison on Robben Island to this day.

For 14 years the blacks suffered more or less in silence.

Soweto

Then in 1976 some students at Soweto (a black town outside Johannesburg) protested against a recent government announcement that their secondary school maths and social studies must be taught in Afrikaans rather than English. The police once again opened fire. Two students were killed, many others injured.

The incident provoked a nationwide uprising. The protests lasted for months. The authorities managed to put it down only after nearly six hundred blacks had been killed and over two thousand injured.

Signs of hope, signs of despair

In 1978 South Africa gained a new prime minister, Mr P W Botha. He declared, 'A white monopoly of power is untenable in the Africa of today,' adding, 'Apartheid is a recipe for permanent conflict.'

Four years later he set up a new parliament. It involved three houses, one for whites, one for 'coloureds' and one for Asians living in South Africa. But as everyone observed, no blacks were represented.

P W Botha created black councils to run their townships. He also allowed skilled blacks to live in the cities. This was apparently not enough for those who had suffered so much. Blacks campaigned against both the councils and the new three-house parliament. Most 'coloureds' and Asians did not vote when the elections were held.

On the day the new parliament opened in 1984, protests began. Those who did co-operate with Botha's government — black policemen, mayors and councillors — were hounded by black saboteurs, murdered, beaten, and their homes burned to the ground.

Mandela still in prison

In 1986 Botha's government responded by promising to free Nelson Mandela if he would renounce violence. Mandela promised only that his followers would 'suspend' violence as long as the state suspended its violence. Botha refused to free him, and instead sought the help of Chief Buthelezi. The chief refused to co-operate unless Nelson Mandela was set free.

In June the Prime Minister declared that South Africa was living under a state of emergency. His government is said to have imprisoned thousands more blacks.

The Christian view

True Christianity condemns any sort of discrimination or prejudice against another human being or group of human beings.

Building on Jesus's teaching, 'Love your neighbour as

Jesus's teaching

yourself,' St Paul and St Peter (the leaders of the early church) made it quite clear that just as God loves everyone equally, so must we. St Peter said,

> The truth that I have now come to realise is that God does not have any favourites, but that anybody of any nationality who fears God and does what is right is acceptable to him.
>
> (Acts of the Apostles chapter 10, verses 34f, Jerusalem Bible)

St Paul

St Paul, writing to the Christian church in Galatia, declared that anyone who becomes part of the Christian body does away with any racial or sexual barriers.

> You have all clothed yourselves in Christ, and there are no more distinctions between Jew and Greek, slave and free, male and female, but all of you are one in Christ Jesus.
>
> (Letter to the Galatians chapter 3, verses 27f, JB)

In the centuries that followed, Christian leaders continued to defend the rights of minorities and insist on the solidarity of all human beings. As we have seen, Pope Clement VI used all his authority in a vain attempt to stop the persecution of Jews in the fourteenth century. In the twentieth century Pope John XXIII sent a letter to all the world's Catholics on the subject of 'Peace on Earth'. In it he declared:

Citizens of the world

1 Every human being has the right to freedom of movement and of residence within the confines of his own country; and, when there are just reasons for it, the right to emigrate to other countries and take up residence there. The fact that one is a citizen of a particular State does not detract in any way from his membership of the human family as a whole, nor from his citizenship of the world community.

Equal in dignity

2 The conviction that all men are equal by reason of their natural dignity has been generally accepted. Hence racial discrimination can in no way be justified . . . This calls, above all, for the elimination of every trace of racialism, and the consequent recognition of the principle that all States are by nature equal in dignity.

Christian leaders have also insisted that loving others as you love yourself involves loving men and women of other faiths as well as of different skin-colour or nationality. In 1964 Pope John XXIII's successor, Pope Paul VI, visited Bombay.

Young people enjoying each others' company regardless of each others' colour

There, addressing representatives of the non-Christian religions, he said:

> Man must meet man, nation meet nation, as brothers and sisters, as children of God. In this mutual understanding and friendship, in this sacred communion, we must also begin to work together to build the common future of the human race.

In the light of this clear teaching, how should Christians respond to racism?

1 Christian responses to Hitler

Niemöller

In Hitler's Germany the true Christian response was clear and extremely dangerous. Many Christians, afraid for their very lives, preferred to look the other way when persecution came to the Jews. Two brave men who did not were Martin Niemöller and Dietrich Bonhoeffer, both Protestant clergymen.

Martin Niemöller knew the risks he was taking in opposing Hitler. 'Contrary to what we may desire,' he wrote in 1933, 'a fundamental stand is required of us, whether we find it agreeable or not.' He met Hitler face to face and openly disagreed with him. Hitler soon took his revenge. That same evening members of the Nazi secret police arrived at his home and ransacked it. A few days later a bomb exploded in the house, setting fire to part of the roof.

Niemöller was arrested five times. Finally he was charged with treason. The judges acquitted him. As he left the court he was arrested and taken to a concentration camp. He remained Hitler's prisoner for the next eight years, until the American forces liberated him in 1945.

Bonhoeffer

Dietrich Bonhoeffer was less fortunate. Imprisoned in Berlin for his part in the attempt to assassinate Adolf Hitler, he refused to give way to self-pity, pointing out that Niemöller had been jailed far longer. 'Please harbour no regrets for me,' he wrote. 'Martin has suffered nearly seven years of it.' In July 1944 he and some of his fellow conspirators against Hitler were hanged.

2 The response to apartheid

Many people outside South Africa decided that the best way to force the Botha regime to change its policy towards blacks was by economic and cultural sanctions.

Economic sanctions

Economic sanctions involve simply refusing to trade with a country. South African diamonds, oranges, gold would be denied markets abroad. At the same time such vital commodities as oil and armaments would no longer be sold to the South Africans. And banks outside South Africa would cease to offer foreign capital and loans to the country.

Cultural sanctions

Cultural sanctions involve for example cutting off sporting contacts with the country. South African athletes would be denied the opportunity to compete in, say, the Olympic Games or the British Commonwealth Games. Rugby teams and cricket elevens would no longer play against their South African opponents. Similarly, foreign pop groups or ballet companies would refuse to perform before South African audiences.

Objections to sanctions

Three objections have been made to these sanctions. First, to apply economic sanctions may well damage the economies of those countries which apply them. Some of the poorer countries of Africa desperately need to trade with

South Africa, however much they abhor apartheid. To refuse to trade with the South Africans could spell ruin. The South Africans can also fight back, denying valuable (sometimes vital) goods and services to those poorer countries.

Secondly, some Christians have said that economic sanctions harm black South Africans even more than white. If there is no market abroad for South African goods, the black labourer who produces them will be thrown out of work. Nevertheless, black leaders in South Africa, such as the Anglican Archbishop of Johannesburg, Desmond Tutu, insist that sanctions must still be applied, for the temporary sufferings of the black communities will seem to them as nothing if sanctions can help to bring an end to apartheid. Nelson Mandela's wife Winnie has said that there can be no real change in South Africa 'until business takes the side of freedom'.

Thirdly, it is argued that the best way to change the South African system of discrimination is not to cut off all trade, sporting and cultural contacts but to keep in touch, culturally and economically, so as to continue to try to persuade the rulers of South Africa to change. Otherwise the white leaders of South Africa may move into a position in which they no longer listen to anyone from the outside world.

3 The defence of sanctions

Apartheid is expensive

Apartheid is an expensive luxury. To keep the vast majority of a country in subject conditions and in racially separate communities requires an army of oppression, which must be paid for. International trade helps to pay for it. As John Vorster, a former South African prime minister, once said, 'Each bank loan, each new investment, is a brick in the wall of our continued existence.'

In addition, white managers in South Africa live in a state of deep anxiety. They fear black strikes, black sabotage, black violence. Sanctions diminish the wealth of a country, making these means of repression harder and harder to sustain. The privileges of the white leadership become enormously expensive. Small wonder that under the impact of international sanctions many South African businesspeople have made journeys outside their country to try to come to terms with the leaders of the banned African National Congress.

Next, sanctions demonstrate that the outside world, and in

Coming to terms with the ANC

particular that part of it led by whites, appreciates the needs and hopes of black South Africa. At present the leadership of the African National Congress is committed to non-racialism, to a democracy in which whites and blacks have an equal part. If the white world continues to support white South Africa culturally and economically, will that commitment to equality disappear as the rage of black people or a thirst for revenge emerges?

Self-interest

Lastly, sheer self-interest may well urge the rest of the world to side with black South Africa rather than its present white masters. After all, many people think, repression of the huge majority of that country cannot continue for ever. Eventually the majority will take power. The outside world needs the friendship of that majority.

A revolution in South Africa could come. As Nelson Mandela's friend Anthony Sampson puts it (in his book *Black and Gold: Tycoons, Revolutionaries and Apartheid*, Hodder and Stoughton 1987), 'the interest of the West must lie in making that revolution as bloodless and manageable as possible; in preserving the continuity of human rights, the respect for law and civilised values; and in making their own links with a future non-racial or black government.'

After the Soweto disturbances, foreign investors began to fear that in a South Africa torn with strife their money was no longer safe. In 1985 the huge American Chase Manhattan Bank mounted a campaign alongside other foreign bankers to cease lending money to the country until Mr Botha introduced new reforms and brought peace to his country.

International banking

Chase Manhattan Bank had actually led international bankers in investing in South Africa after the Sharpeville shootings. By July 1985 they felt that the unrest in that country made their risks unacceptable. Other banks drew the same conclusions. By the end of the following year most other United States investors had pulled much of their business out of South Africa. Their leaders began to build up contacts with the leadership of the African National Congress.

Moral considerations

How moral are these business decisions? Sir Timothy Bevan, chairman of Barclays Bank in 1986 when it began to pull out of South Africa, admitted that he regarded apartheid as 'unchristian and untenable'. He added: 'There cannot be a situation where a businessman says, "I base all my business on moral considerations." Equally, you cannot run a business without morality.'

4 Political prisoners and Amnesty International

Another persecuted group in today's world is made up of political prisoners or 'prisoners of conscience'.

Amnesty International is the chief hope for those unjustly detained. Amnesty was started by three British Christians (a Quaker, a Catholic and an Anglican) in 1961 as an attempt to draw people's attention to the fact that throughout the world thousands of men and women are in prison, not because they have committed any crime but because of their political or religious beliefs.

Prisoners of conscience

These people are known as prisoners of conscience. Prisoners of conscience may well have been imprisoned simply for their beliefs, colour, sex or religion. They are men and women who have neither used violence nor tried to persuade others to do so. Some, in fact, are held solely because they object to military service. Many of them have been tortured and subjected to degrading punishment. Some are threatened with execution. Amnesty seeks their release.

Napoleon Ortigoza

Here is one example of a prisoner of conscience. Napoleon Ortigoza, jailed in Paraguay since 1962, is the longest serving political prisoner in Latin America. As a cavalry captain in the Paraguayan army he became convinced that the government of General Alfredo Stroesser needed removing. Arrested without warning, he was accused of plotting the downfall of Stroesser and of murdering a military cadet. A farcical trial found him guilty and sentenced him to death. Although the sentence was later commuted to 25 years' imprisonment, he is still in jail.

Ten women prisoners

Equally unjust has been the treatment of a sad group of ten women prisoners held in Ethiopia. Five of them belong to the family of the late Emperor Haile Selassie, deposed in 1974 when the country became a republic. The others include a journalist named Martha Kumsa, who worked for a Christian radio station in Ethiopia, and Tsehai Tolessa, wife of the general secretary of the Mekane Jesus Church (who himself has not been seen since 1979).

The oldest of these prisoners is Haile Selassie's daughter Tenagnework, imprisoned like her four daughters since 1974. All five are ill, Tenagnework with a stomach ulcer and rheumatism, and one daughter is partially paralysed. None of the ten women has any plans to overthrow or attack the government. All ten have friends in Britain who would take them in. In May 1988 seven of these women were unexpectedly released.

These are the kinds of prisoners Amnesty works for. Amnesty is not concerned with these prisoners' views, but simply with campaigning for their release.

Today 500,000 individuals belong to Amnesty International. Supporters and subscribers are found in 160 countries, organised into local groups. Whenever Amnesty learns of a prisoner who may be detained for political reasons or on grounds of conscience, its team of investigators sets out to find the truth.

Leonid Volvosky

Thich Nu Tri Hai

If the prisoner is considered to be unjustly detained, he or she is 'adopted' by Amnesty. So Amnesty adopted a Soviet Jew named Leonid Volvosky, sentenced by the Russians in 1985 to three years' imprisonment for circulating Jewish literature and working for human rights. A Buddhist nun and peace-worker named Thich Nu Tri Hai was adopted after the Vietnamese put her in prison in Ho Chi Minh City without trial in 1984.

Once a prisoner has been adopted by Amnesty, its members in other countries begin petitioning and writing to the authorities on his or her behalf. Prison officials and cabinet ministers are besieged with letters. Press releases, newspaper articles, appeals, demonstrations, all gain wide publicity for the prisoner. Prisoners become public concerns, and in the end they are sometimes released.

Torture end execution

Amnesty International has two other specific aims: to have torture and executions totally banned throughout the world. More than 100 countries still kill prisoners, by shooting, decapitating, stoning, electrocuting, lethally injecting or hanging them. And in spite of international agreements outlawing torture, in over 160 countries these agreements are ignored. Repeatedly Amnesty finds out what is happening and, to change the situation, publishes detailed, factual reports condemning those countries.

Amnesty's tactics can work. For instance, in 1987 Amnesty accused the Chinese police of systematically torturing prisoners — by giving them electric shocks, by beating them, by suspending them with their arms tied behind their backs, by handcuffing them so tightly that their flesh was cut to the bone, by forcing them to crouch in little box-like rooms.

At first the Chinese denied the accusations. But soon the chief public prosecutor admitted that between January and

June 1987 the 'human rights' of 2,035 persons had been 'violated'. He promised that this would stop.

More possible solutions

Danger of hatred breeding more hatred

What are the answers to racial discrimination, hatred and prejudice? They must be found. Otherwise the danger of increasing racial tension is very real. If a group remains disadvantaged and harassed for too long, its members become outsiders, hostile and separate. Hatreds develop; and hatreds breed more hatreds.

1 What can the ordinary person do?

Student action

Barclays' decision to pull out from South Africa was influenced by the action of students. Banks woo students. To gain student business the banks offer them free banking services, and sometimes even cash grants. Their hope is that eventually these students will become successful earners and stay with the bank that courted them in their student days.

Recognising this, the National Union of Students mounted a powerful campaign against Barclays Bank because of its involvement with apartheid. The bank reconsidered its whole attitude to South Africa.

This is one example of how a group of apparently ordinary people can have a powerful moral effect if they will act decisively. Similarly, international sporting sanctions have forced the white South Africans to accept multiracial sport.

Individual attitudes also matter in counteracting prejudice and discrimination. Racist jokes may appear harmless. In truth they reinforce racist attitudes, making them seem acceptable rather than harmful. Those of us who make it clear that we find such jokes unacceptable, and indeed consciously set ourselves to disagree politely when anyone expresses racist opinions, are doing something positive to change the climate of opinion for the better.

2 Positive discrimination

'Positive discrimination' is one suggested solution. 'Positive discrimination' involves giving preference, for jobs for example, to those who are apparently disadvantaged by their race — provided that the applicants for the jobs are actually able to do them.

That proviso is important. Quite obviously someone who cannot speak English well enough would be unsuitable as, say, a cashier at a supermarket or a telephonist. So further suggestions are that priority should be given to paying for special facilities to teach English, not just to young immigrants who find it difficult but also to their parents.

Racist

There are some who consider positive discrimination to be 'racist' in itself. Others disagree, asserting that this view is based on a misunderstanding of what positive discrimination is all about. In truth, far from being racist, it is about changing the balance of power, which is at the heart of racism itself.

3 More blacks in power

Local authority staff

Next, it has been frequently suggested that those who run our local authorities should make sure that their staff includes a sufficient number of black employees at all levels.

If we are finally to see the end of discrimination, this idea needs to be carried much further. With Britain's large black population it is obviously absurd that in the 1987 general election only four black people were elected to our House of Commons. That this is changing is a hopeful sign pointing towards an eventual lessening of discrimination here. But the process must go much further. To help to put an end to racial discrimination we need many more black MPs.

MPs

Black persons in positions of power at all levels in society would also help to ensure that open discrimination was no longer acceptable. For instance, they would join the white opponents of prejudice and racism in threatening to remove government contracts from firms which demonstrate racial discrimination in their employment practices. When this was done in America, the businesspeople running such firms soon changed their habits.

4 Holding all peoples in high esteem

The law may make people stop behaving in an openly discriminating way. It cannot change people's minds. If a white person is forced reluctantly to employ a black person and still resents the idea, the relationship between employer

The leader of the British Labour party with the black MPs elected to Parliament in 1987

and employee starts off on a difficult footing.

Positions commanding respect

What will help to change such attitudes is to see more and more black men and women in positions that most of us admire or respect. The more black policemen, black clergymen, black bank managers we seen, the more we shall cease to feel either superior (because we are white) or discriminated against (because we are black).

Today there are not many black people occupying senior

Top jobs

positions in the British police force or sitting as British high court judges. Happily, there are black television newsreaders. There are respected black actors and actresses. There are more and more black head teachers. We have black pop singers and models.

Glamorous jobs

The more these men and women in top and glamorous jobs become part of the nation's way of life, the quicker prejudice and discrimination could begin to disappear.

What sort of world do we want?

The separation of one group of persons from another is not absolutely wrong in all circumstances. For instance, families live closely together and, if they are happy families, create a warm relationship which those outside the family cannot share.

Again, different groups of people have their own ways of living and need communities that understand and support these habits of life. Jews build synagogues to worship in and they eat meat from animals killed only according to Jewish rules. The result in Britain is that, while mixing happily with the predominantly Christian community, Jews have tended to live closely together, with their own Jewish butchers serving their own special needs.

Close communities serve special needs

No aspect of this kind of separation should make one person feel inferior or superior to another. So long as the different groups in our society are not cut off from each other, they enrich each other. A recent guide to London restaurants reveals in its little field exactly how rich we are in the many cultures that have come to Britain. In all our big cities, Indian, Greek, Chinese, Italian, even Polish food tempts the adventurous eater. Life is better, more enjoyable, like that.

Not necessarily exclusive

Tightly knit groups need not exclude others, once the essential solidarity of the human race is accepted. It is possible both to be proud of the environment and culture in which you live and still to thrive beyond its limited sphere. Dangerous tendencies occur only when a group of people becomes cut off from the benefits of belonging to our nation as a whole.

Three possibilities for the future

1 'Blacks go home'

A former Ulster MP, Enoch Powell, once said that immigrants in Britain formed an 'alien wedge' in our society. He suggested that they should be encouraged to go back home.

But where is 'home' for all those black people actually born in Britain?

2 'A melting pot'

A popular song of the sixties described the world as a 'melting pot', producing 'coffee-coloured people'. If this were so, eventually there might be a blurring of every cultural or religious distinction between cultures in one country. Sikhs might cease to wear turbans. The festivals, customs, dress of Muslims, Jews, Hindus might be forgotten. We should, as a result, lose all the pleasures of learning from and about other cultures. Our world would become far less rich.

3 'Integration'

This is a difficult notion, but worth understanding. Someone integrated into a new community does not lose his or her old roots. People can move freely from one environment to another. A young woman may be at home both in the local pub and in the local Hindu temple. A man may wear his turban with his bus conductor's badge pinned on it, instead of the usual uniform. A Jew may well call on his or her neighbour for a Christmas drink.

It is a wonderful goal. To work towards it demands tolerance, understanding, friendship, and a willingness to love your neighbour as you love yourself.

Useful addresses

Amnesty International British Section, 5 Roberts Place, off Bowling Green Lane, London EC1R 0EJ (tel 01–251 8371)

The British Defence and Aid Fund for Southern Africa, Unit 22, The Ivories, Northampton Street, London N1 2HX (tel 01–354 1462)

British Refugee Council, Bondway House, 3 Bondway, London SW8 1SJ (tel 01–582 6922)

Commission for Racial Equality, Elliot House, 10–12 Allington Street, London SW1E 5EH (tel 01–828 7022)
Commonwealth Institute, Kensington High Street, London W8 6NJ (tel 01–603 4535)
The Runnymede Trust, 178 North Gower Street, London NW1 2NB (tel 01–387 8943), publishes monthly bulletins monitoring race relations in Britain.
Copies of the Race Relations Act 1976 and the Code of Practice on Race Relations 1984 are available from the Industrial Society, 3 Carlton House Terrace, London SW1 5DG (tel 01–839 4300).

Questions and coursework

1 In Jesus's time and in his own land two groups of people greatly disliked each other; one group was known as the Samaritans, and the other group was known as the ....
2 What is the word we use to describe unthinking hatred of other people?
3 What do racists believe?
4 Give the date when Britain's Race Relations Act was passed.
5 When the habits or laws of a society deny to groups of people their normal rights, we call this ....
6 How many immigrants from Bangladesh live in Britain?
7 What was the name of the ruler of Germany between 1933 and 1945?
8 What was the title of the book written by that German in 1924?
9 What do we call a Jewish place of worship?
10 The South African word for 'separation' or 'apartness' is ....
11 Give the name of the black South African leader sentenced to life imprisonment in 1962.
12 Christianity condemns any kind of discrimination or ....
13 Christian leaders follow Jesus in insisting that you should love others as you love ....
14 Who sent a letter to all the world's Catholics on the subject of 'Peace on Earth'?

15 Give the name of one German Christian leader who opposed Adolf Hitler
16 In 1961 three British Christians started an organisation called ....
17 Name one prisoner of conscience.
18 In this chapter we have by no means discussed every kind of prejudice. Give an example of the way prejudice in our society operates against women.
19 What is a ghetto?
20 What is the difference between a prejudiced person and a racist?
21 In your own words, tell the story of the 'good Samaritan', and give three reasons why the story is important today.
22 From your own experience give an example of prejudice.
23 Name one country which separates people by their colour.
24 What is your understanding of 'racial prejudice'? Using newspapers, find an example of racial prejudice, try to give reasons for it and say how you would deal with the problem.
25 Describe a prejudiced person.
26 Trace the history of apartheid in South Africa and give your views on the problem today.
27 Imagine you are Martin Niemöller. Adolf Hitler has demanded to see you because he is furious with you, since you have been telling the church that his treatment of the Jews and Gypsies cannot be justified. Write the conversation between yourself and Hitler.
28 What are your views about economic and cultural sanctions against South Africa?
29 What is your understanding of 'positive discrimination'? Give an example and say whether you think the concept is acceptable.
30 You are a young Indian mother who has just moved into an area where there is much racial prejudice and discrimination:
(a) write an article for the local newspaper highlighting the many areas of injustice you have found;
(b) write a Christian response to the article.

31 And all must love the human form,
In heathen, Turk or Jew,
Where Mercy, Love and Pity dwell,
There God is dwelling too. (William Blake)

Comment.

32 Read the following newspaper cutting (from *The Times*, 4 September 1987), and then write a speech in defence of Mrs Moore.

Equality ruling for job-hunter

Married women with children should be treated as equals with single job-hunters, an industrial tribunal ruled yesterday after awarding a woman £250 damages because of sexual discrimination.

Mrs Jacqueline Moore, aged 28, was rejected for a place on a management training scheme by Clarks, the shoe company, despite being suitably qualified, because she was married, with a child.

She said at a Bristol tribunal she was told she could not be appointed to the graduate training post because of her settled domestic background. Mrs Moore, of Oakington, Cambridgeshire, said she had been prepared to move about the country.

Mrs Moore, a graduate in humanities and social studies, said she fought the case to establish a principle and was now a temporary worker at a personnel agency.

Mr Jeremy Baker, a development manager with Clarks, told the tribunal: "A reasonable employer could not expect someone with a young family to up and move all over the country at very short notice.

2 Our Rich World and Our Poor Neighbours

Lessons from the Bible

In the name of God the Bible speaks extremely harshly about people who harm, ill-treat or cheat the poor and needy:

> Listen to this, you who trample on the needy
> and try to suppress the poor people of the country,
> you who say, 'When can we sell our corn
> and market our wheat?
> Then, by lowering the bushel, raising the shekel,
> by swindling and tampering with the scales,
> we can buy up the poor for money,
> and the needy for a pair of sandals,
> and get a price even for the sweepings of the wheat.'
> God swears it by the pride of Jacob,
> 'Never will I forget a single thing that you have done.'
> (Amos chapter 8, verses 4 to 7, JB)

Love your neighbour as yourself

Jesus put this very clearly too. He condemned the greedy and selfish. And to those who wanted to follow him he said that the two rules of a Christian life were, 'Love the Lord your God with all your heart, with all your soul, with all your strength and with all your mind; and your neighbour as yourself.' (Luke chapter 10, verse 27)

Both of these two commands are equally important. To love God involves also loving all of God's children on earth. So one of Jesus's first followers, St John, poured scorn on people who claimed to love God while refusing to help out people in need.

> If a man who was rich enough in this world's goods
> saw that one of his brothers was in need,
> but closed his heart to him,

how could the love of God be living in him?
My children, our love is not to be just words or mere talk,
but something real and active.

(1 John chapter 3, verses 17f, JB)

The needy today

There are millions of people in today's world whose needs are so great as to threaten their very lives.

The *Sunday Times* on 30 August 1987 reported: 'Children are dying of hunger in remote villages in the eastern state of Orissa as India's worst drought in a hundred years begins to take its toll.'

Drought in Orissa

The report continued:

> Local politicians and voluntary workers estimate that at least 500 children are dead already in the worst affected area near the town of Kashipur. They warn that at least another 1,000 will die if nothing is done to provide food in the next two weeks.
>
> Famine conditions prevail in at least three districts of Orissa state, and in hundreds of villages people have been living on seeds and roots for the past two months.

The author of that report, Tavleen Singh, described conditions in one village.

> 'Gahing Manjhi, eight, has been dying for four months. His body is reduced to a thin covering of skin over a pitifully small frame, he can no longer walk and when he tries to speak all that comes out is a sort of whimper. He lives on a diet of crushed mango seeds and wild leaves boiled into gruel. There has been no food grain in the village for two months . . .
>
> Across the road in the village of Deypore Daigan conditions are even worse. Mithila Mahi, 22, died because she could no longer survive on the village's staple diet of bamboo shoots and leaves. She left two children aged six and four months.

Staple diets

Comparing a diet of crushed mango seeds or bamboo shoots and wild leaves with what we often take for granted in Britain is revealing. Our midday meal could well be fish and chips or, if we are vegetarian, veggieburgers and chips. In

Starving children in the Third World

the evening many of us tuck into steak and kidney pie with boiled potatoes, or maybe a chicken pilaff followed by ice cream. All day long some of us 'keep ourselves going' with crisps and sweets, with chocolate or biscuits. In offices there are traditional tea breaks between the main meals.

At least, normal diets in Asia and Africa are much healthier. The rice cakes and boiled rice dishes of Bangladesh: the maize or millet porridge and the cassavas and meat stews of West Africa and Bolivia; the stewed meat, herbs and locust beans eaten in East Africa are all far less saturated in oils, fats and sugar than the average British diet.

The problem of poverty and starvation lies not in the staple diets of those and other developing countries. People die there because there is simply not enough to eat.

1 Diseases

Kwashiorkor

Two fatal diseases in particular attack children who are starving. One is kwashiorkor. Kwashiorkor generally attacks children aged two or three. The child's hair turns red and perhaps falls out, the stomach swells absurdly, the muscles waste away. Even deadlier is the disease known as marasmus. Marasmus attacks infants, often in their first year. A child suffering from marasmus grows thinner and thinner, until his or her body looks like a skeleton with skin stretched tightly across it. The baby's face looks like that of an old man. The cause of both killing diseases is simply and solely lack of food.

Marasmus

2 How much food do we need?

How much food we need depends on our age and what we do. A baby needs only about 800 calories a day. A man whose job requires hard manual work needs around 4,250 calories, whereas those who sit down all day at work need only 2,400. Nutrition experts estimate that growing teenagers require 3,400 calories a day.

Food supplies of the world

So, can the world supply enough food for everyone? The answer is certainly yes. Between 1973 and 1982 the cereals produced throughout the world increased by something like 300 million tonnes. If this grain were distributed fairly among all the nations of the world every single person would eat enough protein and 3,000 calories a day. In addition the earth supplies vegetables, meat, milk and fruit. Yet in the same period that the grain production of the world was so rapidly rising, the number of hungry and starving people doubled.

Many of these are children, such as the ones seen dying by Tavleen Singh. The United Nations International Children's Emergency Commission believes that each year over 15 million children die of hunger. A thousand children a day die in Ethiopia alone. More than 500 million people today are suffering from desperate malnutrition. Eighty million people in India try to live on less than half of the calories they need.

70% of grain is for the rich 20%

The reasons are scandalous. Basically, the rich northern parts of the world take 70 per cent of the world's grain, even though they contain only 20 per cent of the world's population. The other 80 per cent have to try to exist on only 30 per cent of the world's grain.

Many of these poor once held land and fed themselves from it. Richer, more powerful landowners took it from them. In other cases the poor still own land but cannot pay for seeds or fertilisers. Those who live in towns and are out of work simply cannot grow or buy food.

Very often the land is distributed in an extremely unfair way. Take Guatemala for instance. There, 2 per cent of the population owns 80 per cent of the land. Again, in north-east Brazil, the rich live on more than 4,000 calories a day; the poor eat on average only 2,400 calories a day.

3 Natural disasters

Why are so many people so poor? World poverty cannot by any means always be blamed on the rulers of those countries whose people suffer it or on the people themselves.

Natural disasters over which no one yet has control often contribute to starvation. When the rains finally came to India in 1987, they were two months late. Drinking water and fodder for cattle increased; but many summer crops throughout northern India were ruined.

India at that time had emergency stores of wheat amounting to 22 million tonnes. The wheat harvest fell short of its usual capacity by 27 million tonnes.

Floods in Bangladesh

A tragic contrast to India's drought were the floods in nearby Bangladesh, bringing equal misery in 1987. When the monsoons began, the heavy rain brought rivers in both eastern India and Bangladesh to dangerous levels. The

Brahmaputra river, along with the Padma and Mahananda, overflowed. At least 200 people died of diarrhoea and dysentery, and another 700 died from drowning, starvation and other diseases. The flooding caused over £790 million of damage. In 1988 it was even worse, this time leaving well over 1,000 dead and countless more homeless.

4 Civil war

Wars also lead to poverty, especially civil wars within one country.

Conflict in Sudan

When the Western powers withdrew from Africa, they left behind a land many of whose countries contained different tribes and people at odds with each other. Sudan — once controlled by the British — is such a country. Northern Sudan is peopled by Muslims who speak Arabic. To the south live blacks whose culture is far more European. The southern blacks are dominated by the northern Muslims.

In 1955 the southerners revolted. The rebellion lasted 17 years. Peace in 1972 endured only till 1983, when a group called the Sudan People's Liberation Army (SPLA) took up arms again against the northerners. The SPLA demanded an end to the Muslim code under which they were ruled. The north refused, at a cost to themselves of one million dollars a day in fighting off the southerners. As a result the economy of the Sudan is in a terrible state. It need not be. Oil has been discovered in the upper Nile, but no one develops it because of the war. And, tragically, the country's whole civilisation is at risk, as local warlords use the civil war as a pretext to pursue their own vendettas and kill their enemies.

Sudan simply cannot afford such a war. The United Nations in 1975 included Sudan (along with 17 other African nations) among the least developed in the world. In 1976 Sudan's debts to the rest of the world were a colossal $1,268 million.

Lost opportunity

Yet during its brief years of peace many considered that Sudan could become the 'breadbasket' of the Arab world. In 1976 Britain and other members of the European Common Market (EEC) made development loans available to Sudan. The following year the other Arab countries and the World Bank gave Sudan massive cash grants. Denmark gave valuable aid between 1976 and 1978, particularly in developing Sudanese education. In 1978 the Swedish government decided to write off Sudan's debts. Russian aid to Sudan by 1973 had amounted to $65 million.

The anarchy prevailing today in Sudan, as a result of the war restarting, threatens to make much of this aid ultimately useless.

5 One-crop economies

Other countries are poor simply because they have to rely on one fragile export. The reasons for this are complex and varied, but the West must bear a heavy responsibility in often forcing these countries into a straightjacket with loans, trade agreements and so on, which may be based on short-sighted self-interest rather than the real interests of the country in question.

Zambia's copper

Zambia derives 95 per cent of its export earnings from selling copper. And as a landlocked country, Zambia depends on the goodwill of neighbouring countries to export at all.

Between 1964, when Zambia became independent, and 1973, the price of copper on international markets was high enough for the Zambians to obtain loans to develop their country. Then the price of copper slumped, and Zambia was in deep financial trouble. At the same time the civil war in Rhodesia (now Zimbabwe) frequently spread over into Zambia through raids across the border.

The international community rallied round, with loans technical assistance, and (from China) help in building the vital TANZAM railway. Britain sent teachers. However, none of Zambia's troubles would have been so stark if the country had not been so heavily dependent on selling one product, copper. Similar problems face other Third World countries. Gambia and Mauritius are virtually dependent on the price for which they can sell groundnuts and sugar.

Brazil's sugar

Brazil has the same problem, depending almost totally on sugar. Miguel Arraes, former governor of Pernambuco in north-east Brazil, has declared that 'The enormous strip of cultivated land in north-east Brazil is one of the most fertile areas in the world. It is nine times as large as the cultivated land of Japan, which feeds 100 million people. But on our land we grow only sugar cane and some subsistence products in quantities far below what the 23 million people need who live in the region.'

Miguel Arraes added that the problem was made much worse because the crops belonged not to the whole population, but to half-a-dozen rich landowners. Small wonder that in north-east Brazil many men die of 'old age' when they are only 28.

6 Corruption and mismanagement

Governments are frequently to blame in creating conditions that keep their people starving.

The fate of emergency food in Bangladesh

Between 1976 and 1981, half of all the emergency food sent as aid to the starving went to Egypt, Indonesia, India and Bangladesh, much of it rice and wheat. In Bangladesh 90 per cent of this was taken over by the government and sold at subsidised prices through a special system of rationing.

A third of this was specified as food for the police, the civil service and the army. Another third went to reasonably prosperous people living in the towns, whose support the government needed. The final third was meant for the poor in the countryside. Much of it never reached them and was sold on the black market. The sale of emergency food in 1976–77 brought the government of Bangladesh no less than one-fifth of its income.

7 Too many children?

Every five days a million babies are born in the world. Most of them are born to the world's poor. Those countries least able to feed their people have the highest birth rate.

Support for the old

The reason for this apparently absurd situation is that the poor desperately need to bear children. In a land where most children die of undernourishment extremely young, unless parents continue to breed more there will be no adults left to support them when they themselves (if they are lucky) grow old. Hunger and the threat of starvation cause high birth rates, which in turn contribute to hunger and starvation.

More from the Bible

Before blaming the very poorest on earth for having too many children (instead of trying to do something about the poverty that makes them have more children than they can support), we should ponder some words at the very beginning of the Bible.

The first chapter of the book of Genesis (the very first book in the Bible) describes the creation of the universe by God in a way that emphasises how rich and good it all is.

God is pictured creating rivers and seas, vegetation, fruit trees, birds and fishes, cattle and wild beasts.

Then comes the creation of men and women. God is shown sharing with us some of his own glory. He makes us 'in his likeness'. And then all the riches of the universe are put at our disposal.

> God said, 'Let us make man in our own image, in the likeness of ourselves, and let them be masters of the fish of the sea, the birds of heaven, the cattle, all the wild beasts and all the reptiles that crawl upon the earth'.
>
> God created man in the image of himself,
> in the image of God he created him,
> male and female he created them.
>
> God blessed them, saying to them, 'Be fruitful and multiply, fill the earth and conquer it. Be masters of the fish of the sea, the birds of heaven and all living animals on the earth.' God said, 'See, I give you all the seed-bearing plants that are upon the whole earth and all the trees with seed-bearing fruit: this shall be your food. To all wild beasts, all birds of heaven and all living reptiles on the earth I give all the foliage of plants for food.' And so it was. God saw all that he had made, and indeed it was very good.
>
> (Genesis chapter 1, verses 26 to 31, JB)

If you accept this picture of how the world should be run, there are questions that are worth asking:

- Should people be forbidden to obey God's command 'Be fruitful and multiply', simply because we have failed to care properly for the rich world God has given us?
- Is there anything in this picture of God's creation which suggests that some human beings should take most of the earth's goods for themselves and keep them from other human beings, even to the extent of letting those other men, women and children 'created in the image of God' die of starvation?

Misuse of our world

The following extract is from an article which appeared in the *Observer* on 30 August 1987.

Between the meeting of the United Nations Conference

Destruction of production land

and 1987, productive land the size of 12 European countries had been turned to bowls of dust. In consequence more than 850 million people are at risk in the world. Since no less than one-third of the entire surface of the world (leaving out the oceans) is at risk, maybe 1,200 million will be starving by the end of the twentieth century.

> Ten years ago this weekend a special UN Conference opened at which the world solemnly agreed a package of measures to halt the spread of the deserts by the year 2000. Since then virtually nothing has been done. Rich countries have failed to provide the money they promised; poor countries have failed to show any interest, even when their own croplands disappeared into the sand. The hundreds of millions of people most affected, always among the poorest and most disorganised, have been powerless to make their Governments fulfil their undertakings.
>
> The causes of this massive loss of ground remain, as the world agreed ten years ago, overcultivation, overgrazing, and the cutting down of trees. The solutions then resolved upon remain technically practicable, and far cheaper than the cost of losing the land. The urgency is now infinitely greater. The world must act upon what it formally adopted ten years ago — and fast — before the very foundations of our civilisation crumble in the sand.

'No civilisation has set about consuming its future with such enthusiasm as our own,' the newspaper concluded.

But the picture in Genesis which we have just read, describing how God gives us the riches of world, nowhere suggests that we have the right to destroy those riches. In fact, the Bible specially says that the foliage of plants belongs to other creatures, not ourselves. In so savagely destroying plants and trees, we are endangering other parts of God's living creation, the animal kingdom.

1 Pollution

We would be foolish to suppose that it is only in the poorer countries that men and women do not properly care for the land and the rivers they have inherited and the food these produce. As Wendell Berry wrote (in *The Unsettling of America: Culture and Agriculture*, San Francisco 1977), 'It is one of the miracles of science and hygiene that the germs that used to be in our food have been replaced by poisons.'

Greenpeace takes action against pollution

Most of these poisons come from the rich industrialised countries of our world.

In 1969, for example, some pest-killing chemicals were leaked into the River Rhine, in Germany. The poison flowed downstream, killing as it went thousands of fish. Some of it spread by sea to faraway Portugal, poisoning edible fish on its shores.

Sea pollution
Air pollution

Alongside sea pollution the developed nations of the world have created great problems with air pollution. Britain is one of the worst offenders here.

Two chemicals, sulphur dioxide and nitrogen oxide, are pumped into the air by our factories and especially by our power stations. Much is then blown over Scandinavia. These chemicals then fall as 'acid rain' (for mingled with rain itself, snow, hail or fog, they transform themselves into poisonous sulphuric and nitric acid, two chemicals deadly to fish and trees).

Over half the Norwegian trout population living in an area of 32,000 square kilometres has been lost. A survey of 1985 found that just over half of all the forests of West Germany had damaged trees, perhaps some 7 per cent of their trees being likely to die.

Poisoning our own rivers

If Britain's factories damage the forests and lakes of other lands, we also pollute our own country. On 3 September 1987 a letter appeared in *The Times* describing a trip down the River Stour.

> **Enjoying rivers**
>
> *From Mr Michael Hughes*
> Sir, On a fund-raising expedition for our little church here, three of my sons and I recently followed the brook that rises in this parish until it joined the Stour, south of Gillingham, and then launched a canoe in which we followed it to the sea at Christchurch.
>
> Above Wimborne the clarity of the water was a tribute to the farmers and the water board, and the fishermen and riparian users were friendly and courteous. Thereafter more and more treated sewage is poured in, and we were told that to drink a mouthful of river water was to guarantee a few days' illness.
>
> One adjoining channel was so black that I could not see my paddle in the water. Is it really sensible to use our rivers as open pipes to the sea, rather than keeping fresh water and foul separate?

2 Solutions

There is some good news. Britain has plans to install cleaner burners in our coal-fired power stations, costing £170 million but also reducing nitrogen oxide fumes by 10 per cent. Again, in Helsinki in 1985 21 countries joined the '30 per cent club', dedicated to reducing their emissions of sulphur dioxide by a third. Other countries are joining in too. And we are all beginning to ask ourselves whether we can go on poisoning our rivers and the sea by using them as some enormous dustbin for our unwanted waste.

Refugees

A special desperately poor group in our world are those known as refugees.

Human beings often cause immense suffering to their fellow men and women, particularly in wartime. Innocent families are forced to flee for their lives, leaving behind their lands, crops, cattle and virtually all they possess. We call these unfortunate people 'refugees'.

Palestinians

Ethiopians

Today there are two million Palestinian refugees as a result of the Arab-Israel conflict which began in 1947. More recently, war in Ethiopia has forced another two million persons to become refugees. In 1962 the United Nations High Commissioner for Refugees estimated that there were altogether 16 million refugees throughout the world, most of them clinging to survival in some of our poorest regions.

1 Not so lucky

Any person arriving in Britain can apply to stay here as a refugee. Not all, however, are accepted. Of the Vietnamese refugees who came here in 1982, about 1,000 were turned away for various reasons. Some associations set up to help refugees (such as the British Refugee Council) have expressed their concern that those awaiting the answer of the Home Office on whether they can stay or not are kept in detention centres (including moored ferries) which remind some of them of their previous sufferings and of the repression from which they are fleeing.

Britain signed the 1951 United Nations convention on refugees, promising to deal sympathetically with people fleeing out of 'a genuine fear of persecution'. But what often happens is that refugees fleeing persecution in their own lands arrive at our airports after they have passed through other countries on the way. Sometimes these refugees are not admitted to Britain but are sent back to these transit countries.

Britain has a legal right to do this. But often it is known that the transit country will immediately send the refugee back to the country he or she first came from — to face renewed persecution or even death.

Sometimes refugees not allowed into our country will do anything, however humiliating, in a desperate attempt to get the decision to expel them reversed. Here is a *Guardian* report of 10 September 1987.

> **Iranian halts jet in asylum protest**
>
> An Iranian who was refused asylum in Britain after arriving from Greece prevented a British Airways jet from taking off at Heathrow airport yesterday by staging a violent protest on board in an attempt to avoid being sent back to Athens.
>
> A British Airways spokeswoman said no one was hurt and no damage was done to the aircraft. The man was detained and is likely to be escorted back to Greece.

2 Christian concern

In his letter called 'Peace on Earth', written to the world's Catholic Christians in 1963, Pope John XXIII spoke of his 'profound sadness' when he considered the growing number of political refugees.

Denial of freedom

Men and women suffering in this way 'show that there are some political regimes which do not guarantee for individual citizens a sufficient sphere of freedom within which their souls are allowed to breathe humanly', the Pope continued; 'in fact, under those regimes even the lawful existence of such a sphere of freedom is either called into question or denied'. He went on to argue that 'that sphere of freedom' is a fundamental right of every member of human society.

Refugees have rights

Refugees, the Pope insisted, 'are persons, and all their rights as persons must be recognized, since they do not lose those rights on losing citizenship of the States of which they are former members.' According to Pope John XXIII, the principles both of human solidarity and of Christian charity require us to make migration of persons from one country to another less painful. 'Among the rights of a human person,' he said, 'there must be included that by which a man may enter a political community where he hopes he can more fittingly provide a future for himself and his dependents.'

3 The Bible on refugees

The ancient Jews had been refugees. Slaves of the ancient Egyptians, cruelly treated, they were led to freedom by Moses.

Moses told them that God was on their side in this march from persecution. He told them that 'God said, "I have seen the miserable state of my people in Egypt. I have heard their appeal to be free of their slave drivers. Yes, I am well aware of their sufferings. I mean to deliver them out of the hands of the Egyptians and bring them up out of that land to a land rich and broad where milk and honey flow."' (Exodus chapter 3, verses 7 to 9)

Exodus

At the same time God made it clear to the Jews that once they came to that rich land they should not forget either that they had once suffered or that the riches of the land were to be shared with others.

They were told to take an offering of the goods of the land to the priest and before God declare:

> The Egyptians ill-treated us, they gave us no peace and inflicted harsh slavery on us. But we called on the God of our fathers. God heard our voice and saw our misery, our toil and oppression; and God brought us out of Egypt with a mighty hand and outstretched arm, with great terror and with signs and wonders.
>
> He brought us here and gave us this land, a land where milk and honey flow.

God told them:

> Then you are to feast on all the good things God has given you, you and your household, and with you the Levite and the stranger who lives among you.
>
> (Deuteronomy chapter 26, verses 5 to 11, JB)

The Jews were to remember the sufferings of their persecution and the terror of being refugees. Now they were rich, God reminded them to share their good things with others.

According to St Matthew's Gospel, as a child Jesus himself and his parents had lived for a time as refugees. King Herod, we are told, wanted to kill him. Overnight his parents left for Egypt and stayed there till Herod was dead. 'Herod was furious when he realised that he had been outwitted, and in Bethlehem and in all the surrounding district he had all the male children killed who were under two years old.' (Matthew chapter 2, verses 13ff, JB)

The Bible on loving the poor, the prisoner and the stranger

In view of the history of the ancient Jews and the infant Jesus, it is not surprising that both taught the need to love the poor. A Jewish hymn to God runs:

> I know God will avenge the wretched
> and see justice done for the poor.
> (Psalm 140, verse 12)

Jewish proverbs

God himself being on the side of the poor, a Jewish proverb declares that to give to the poor is the same as giving to God, adding that God will repay you for what you have done. Another proverb states that:

> A blessing awaits the man who is kindly,
> since he shares his bread with the poor.
> (Proverbs chapter 19, verse 17 and chapter 22, verse 9)

Jesus

Jesus once said that when you give a feast or a party, instead of inviting the rich and anyone else who might repay you (by inviting you back to another party), you should 'invite the poor, the crippled, the lame, the blind. That they cannot pay you back means that you are fortunate, for repayment will be made to you when the virtuous rise again.' (Luke chapter 14, verses 12 to 14)

Jesus too, following the beliefs of the Jews amongst whom he was born, saw loving the poor or the stranger, as well as those suffering sickness or those in prison, as the same as loving God. He explained what God's judgment would be like at the end of the world.

> When the Son of Man comes in his glory, escorted by all the angels, then he will take his seat on the throne of glory. All the nations will be assembled before him and he will separate men one from another as a shepherd separates sheep from goats. He will place the sheep on his right hand and the goats on his left.
>
> Then the King will say to those on his right hand, 'Come, you whom my Father has blessed, take for your heritage the kingdom prepared for you since the foundation of the world. For I was hungry and you gave me food. I was thirsty and you gave me drink; I was a stranger and you made me welcome, naked and you clothed me, sick and you visited me, in prison and you came to see me.'

> Then the virtuous will say to him in reply, 'Lord, when did we see you hungry and feed you; or thirsty and give you drink? When did we see you a stranger and make you welcome; naked and clothe you; sick or in prison and go to see you?' And the King will answer, 'I tell you solemnly, in so far as you did this to one of the least of these brothers of mine, you did it to me.'

With the 'goats' the exact opposite will be the case, according to Jesus. Their refusal to help the poor, hungry, thirsty, imprisoned and strangers will be seen as refusing to help the King himself. 'He will answer them,' said Jesus, '"I tell you solemnly, in so far as you neglected to do this to one of the least of these, you neglected to do it to me." And they will go away to eternal punishment, and the virtuous to eternal life.' (Matthew chapter 25, verses 31 to 46)

God, then, is on the side of the poor, the suffering, the refugee, the starving and the cruelly treated. He requires us to be on their side too.

The Brandt reports

1 North-South

In 1980 the former chancellor of West Germany, Willy Brandt, chaired a group of experts (including Edward Heath, British prime minister from 1970 to 1974, and Shridath Ramphal, Commonwealth secretary-general) who published a report called *North-South. A programme for Survival.*

The report stressed that the north, which owns 90 per cent of the world's manufacturing industry, also has a standard of living 40 times higher than that of the south and possesses four-fifths of the world's income — even though it shelters only a quarter of the world's population. The report pointed out that the percentage of children dying in the south is 10 times that in the north. It observed that the householders and golfers of the United States of America use up as much fertiliser on their courses and gardens as people in India use on everything.

World is inter-united

The Brandt report also pointed out that the world is interdependent. The north needs the south just as much as the south needs the north. If the south grows poorer, then the north grows poorer too, since no one in the developing world has the cash to buy its manufactured goods.

The poor south, the report urged needs:

- more finance;
- decent trading terms;
- enough food to live; and
- help from the rich nations in developing energy.

Every year for the next 20 years, the Brandt commission decided, the rich countries of the world needed to give to the poor countries an extra £2,000 million. Only then would the provision of clean water for the poor, the replanting of their forests and the elimination of such diseases as malaria and worm infections be achieved.

Inspired by Brandt, world leaders met in Mexico in 1981. They talked — but they did not guarantee £2,000 million.

2 Common Crisis

Two years later the Brandt commission produced another, far more alarming report, called *Common Crisis*. The crisis, wrote Willy Brandt, was now far more desperate:

> Our situation is unique,' he declared. 'Never before was the survival of mankind itself at stake; and never before was mankind capable of destroying itself, not only as the possible outcome of a world-wide arms race, but as a result of uncontrolled exploitation and destruction of global resources as well. We may be arming ourselves to death without actually going to war — by strangling our economies and refusing to invest in the future.
>
> (*Common Crisis, North-South: Cooperation for World Recovery*, Pan Books 1983, p9)

Unmanageable debts

By 1982, as the Brandt commission noticed with alarm, the large debts of some East European and developing countries were beginning to prove unmanageable. In consequence, these developing countries were far worse off than they had been ten years previously.

Huge cost of loans

Even then the president of Chile, Salvador Allende, had drawn attention to the absurdity of the Latin American countries being lent $3,900 million and having to repay so much interest that the loan cost Chile altogether $12,800 million. As Salvador Allende had put it in 1972, 'Our region paid out four dollars for every dollar it received.'

Ten years later the exports of such poor countries were still decreasing, and their foreign earnings declining even more. Despite all the appeals of Christian and other leaders, the poor and starving are still with us.

A summary of poverty and wealth in today's world

According to a United Nations estimate, at least 460 million people were seriously underfed in 1974. Another 600 million were on the edge of starvation. Today the situation is worse.

The average annual earnings of people in 31 countries in the world at the beginning of the 1980s were only £140. The citizens of these countries were the poorest on earth. Twenty-one of these countries are in Africa, one is in central America, nine are in Asia. By contrast the 27 richest countries in the world sheltered citizens earning an average of £4,770 a year. (These figures include those who don't work as well as those who do, dividing up the money of the wage-earners amongst all those who depend on them.)

The poor

The rich

In one of the poor countries the chance of a young person being educated is far below that of a young person in a rich country. Bangladesh has one teacher for every 55 pupils. Britain has one for every 20.

Many in the poor countries of the world would not live long enough to benefit from such education, even if it were available. In Latin America four people a minute die of curable diseases, premature old age or simple hunger. That means 5,500 a day, or two million a year.

At the same time 1,000 million people in today's world are estimated to be around 20 years of age. These are the men and women whose children will have doubled the world's population (unless there is some world-wide disaster) by the year AD 2000.

World's population could thrive

And yet responsible agricultural experts tell us that our world can, if properly cultivated, support more than four times its present population.

We are responsible for our world: barren and fertile lands in India

Whose world is it?

On the face of it, the question might seem absurd. The land belongs to those who have control of it. Oil wells belong to their owners. Wealth belongs to the rich nations.

The Bible gives a different answer. The world belongs first of all to God. 'The earth is the Lord's, and everything it holds, the world and all those who dwell in it.' (Psalm 24, verse 1)

We have the world as a gift from God. 'Heaven belongs to the Lord,' says another Psalm, 'earth he has given to man.' (Psalm 115, verse 16)

This is a tremendous gift. It makes us a little like God, says the Bible. God has crowned us with glory and splendour by making us lord over the work of his own hands, setting all things under our feet, 'sheep and oxen, all these, yes, wild animals too, birds in the air, fish in the sea, travelling the paths of the ocean.' (Psalm 8, verses 5 to 8)

God's world

Yet the Bible never suggests that we may exploit the world selfishly. It is still God's world, the world of a God who loves the poor and the outsider.

The Jews developed an extraordinary rule because they believed this. They were told in the Bible never to cut for themselves the whole of a field at harvest time or gather every single grape or fruit from their trees. Something must be left for the poor and the foreigner.

> When you gather the harvest of your land, you are not to harvest to the very end of the field. You are not to gather the gleanings of the harvest. You are neither to strip your vine bare nor to collect the fruit that has fallen in your vineyard. You must leave them for the poor and the stranger.
>
> (Leviticus chapter 19, verses 9f)

Few rich nations or persons in today's world behave like this.

Another rule in the Bible is quite clear and utterly simple. God says, 'Let there be no poor among you.' (Deuteronomy chapter 15, verse 4)

1 Rich and poor

Jesus took these rules even further. The rich should sacrifice all they possess to feed the poor. Once he met a rich man whose life had been spent observing every law in the Bible. According to St Mark's Gospel, 'Jesus looked steadily at him and loved him, and he said, "There is one thing you lack. Go and sell everything you own and give the money to the poor, and you will have treasure in heaven; then come, follow me." But the man's face fell at these words, for he possessed great wealth. Jesus looked round and said to his disciples, "How hard it is for those who have riches to enter the kingdom of God!"' (Mark chapter 10, verses 21 to 23)

Problems for the wealthy

Remember, we are the wealthy of today's world.

2 What can we do?

We can change our life-style. Simply by deciding not to live so selfishly, our example will spread.

If, too, we indulge ourselves a little less — on beer, or sweets, or cigarettes — and give what we save to the world's poor, that is a start at changing their situation. If most of us did this, a huge amount of cash would be available from Britain alone to help the poor.

Jesus said that he had come to earth 'to bring good news to the poor, to proclaim liberty to the captives and to the blind new sight, to set the downtrodden free and to proclaim the Lord's year of favour.' (Luke chapter 4, verse 18)

Christian aid

In the spirit of those words Christians have set up voluntary agencies to collect and channel aid to the needy. One such agency is the Catholic Fund for Overseas Development. Another is simply called 'Christian Aid'. They depend totally on public support.

3 Emergency aid

Natural or man-made disasters create emergencies when thousands of people need food, shelter and water before anything else. Christian Aid raised and spent more than £900,000 on such emergency projects in 1981.

Afghanistan

The following year the civil war in Afghanistan between Islamic forces and Russian troops (begun in 1979) had forced one in every ten Afghans to flee. Most of these refugees had crossed the Khyber Pass into Pakistan, a poor country itself with no hope of supporting the newcomers. The Afghans had managed to bring with them three million sheep, cows and goats; but they desperately needed tents, schooling and medicine. Christian Aid in 1982 managed to send £25,000 towards this.

Altogether Christian Aid spends about 9 per cent of its annual budget on refugees — a total of £940,000 in 1981–82.

The tasks never cease. By 1987 the number of Afghan refugees in Pakistan and Iran had reached five million — one-third of Afghanistan's total population and the largest concentration of refugees in the world.

Mozambique

Meanwhile in Mozambique the long continuing civil war and a savage drought had reduced 4.5 million people to the verge of starvation, thousands lacking anything to eat but roots and clothed only in sacks. In 1987 Christian Aid linked with other voluntary agencies (OXFAM, Save the Children Fund, Help the Aged, the British Red Cross and the Catholic Fund for Overseas Development) to launch a disaster emergency appeal.

Already half-a-million pounds had been sent to the Christian Council of Mozambique. But that body in the summer of 1987 launched an appeal for 2.8 million more — knowing that this kind of emergency aid can be raised only in the rich countries of the world.

4 Long-term aid

Emergency aid is vital; but it does nothing to help the poor to create a new life for themselves.

Voluntary agencies, therefore, increasingly try to concentrate their resources on *helping the poor to help themselves*, supporting many small-scale projects that can be run by local people. This can enable even the very poorest to have some new hope and also some control over their lives.

This policy means trying to put local voluntary agencies (such as the Christian Council of Mozambique mentioned above) in charge of the projects, not governments (which may be corrupt and in any case cannot be trusted at a time of civil war). It means spending more on helping local community organisations and training local people, instead of buying expensive new equipment and machinery.

Gonoshsthaya Kendra project

So, for example, in Bangladesh Christian Aid money (amounting to £80,000 in 1986 and 1987) has been spent on the Gonoshsthaya Kendra project. This is a scheme set up by rural health workers. They have built a factory to manufacture basic drugs which cost much less than medicines imported from abroad. They foster better farming and teaching, as well as small workshops and industries which are slowly bringing more money to the region.

Out of every pound that they raise, the leading voluntary organisations spend around half on such development projects and only around 11p on emergency aid.

Changing people's minds

The voluntary aid societies are not, under British law, allowed to enter party politics. They cannot attack the views of one political party and support those of another.

But they can try to educate public opinion. They use some of their funds to point out, for instance, that the 17 billion dollars a year which it would cost to provide everyone in the world with enough food, water, health care, education and housing is spent *every two weeks* on the world's armaments.

Raising cash

One practical way in which anyone can help is to raise cash for aid. Each year, for instance, Christian Aid sets aside one week in May as 'Christian Aid Week'. During Christian Aid Week teams of volunteers put special envelopes through letter boxes in their neighbourhood, asking people to respond with cash. Later in the week they return to pick up these envelopes, hopefully crammed full of money.

It is simple and effective. In 1985–86 Christian Aid's income was £17 million. About £5.5 million was raised in Christian Aid Week.

Bob Geldof

Sometimes emergencies hugely appeal to the consciences of young people. When the pop star Bob Geldof organised Band Aid and Live Aid the impact was immense.

5 Appealing to governments

Unlike the voluntary aid organisations, Bob Geldof is not prevented by law from tackling the politicians themselves.

As starving Ethiopian refugees were flocking into Sudan, he went to see Dr Baha Idris in the People's Palace, and asked about the government's plans for the famine now knocking at the palace gates.

'Whatever do you mean by that?' asked the urbane and astonished doctor.

'Well, I've just come from Omdurman. There are tens of thousands of people out there with no food and no water. I have seen people collapse from malnutrition,' Geldof responded. To Bob Geldof's surprise, Dr Idris told him, 'There is no famine', and 'We have the situation under control'.

Bob Geldof in Ethiopia

Geldof's reply was: 'Your idea of control seems to be trucking people back out to the desert and dumping them there. But they just walk straight back'. (*Is That It?*, Penguin Books 1986, p315)

We can follow Bob Geldof's example by, for instance, asking our local MPs what their attitude is to aid for the poor.

Influencing governments

Governments, including our own, could be persuaded to spend more on overseas aid. Whereas in 1980 Denmark spent £47 per head of its population on official government aid to developing countries, Britain spent only £18 per head.

Government aid is usually channelled to the poor in one of two ways. The government giving aid may offer it directly to the government of a needy country. About 60 per cent of British government aid is spent in this way. In other cases several donor countries pool their aid and send it to the poor through the World Bank or United Nations funds. About 40 per cent of British government aid is sent in this way.

Government aid versus voluntary aid

There are striking differences between government aid and voluntary aid.

Government aid almost always works through official channels in the poor countries. Voluntary aid usually works through local communities.

Government aid tends to fund large and important schemes, such as new dams, airports or roads. Voluntary aid helps small-scale plans and projects.

Government aid sends highly skilled workers to poor countries. Voluntary aid trains and works through the people of the poor country themselves.

The Brandt reports praised both sorts of aid. But the second report had this to say about the voluntary organisations:

> In many of the aims of poverty-focussed aid, private voluntary organisations of developed and developing countries such as religious organisations, trade unions, CARE, the International Red Cross, Médecins sans frontières. Oxfam, Save the Children and numerous others have amassed valuable and successful experience. In meeting the needs of the poor at local level, in encouraging self-help and participation, in appreciating the social and cultural sensibilities of all the people involved, in circumventing bureaucratic red-tape and getting things done, they have a truly remarkable record.'
>
> (*Common Crisis*, Pan Books, p80)

Volunteers helping to train local communities to help themselves

6 See for yourself

The churches and the Commonwealth have considerable experience of arranging visits from Britain to the poorer countries of the world. Amongst the most profitable and fascinating of these are youth exchanges with a partner group from Africa, the Caribbean or the sub-continent of India.

Groups (preferably small ones) raise their own funds for the visits, often the group from the richer country raising something for the poorer group. Help and advice can be obtained from:

- Christians Abroad,
- the Commonwealth Youth Exchange Council,
- the Methodist World Affairs Secretary, and
- the Central Bureau for Educational Visits and Exchanges

(see page 55 for their addresses).

Voluntary Service Overseas

Many single persons aged between 20 and 65 have seized the opportunity of using their talents to help the developing nations through the organisation known as Voluntary Service Overseas.

VSO needs all sorts of talents: teachers, health workers,

people with experience of factory work and agriculture, of technical trades and engineering. If you have social work experience or business development knowledge, if you have some skills as a community worker or a business adviser, if you are good at crafts — weaving, pottery and so on — the developing world may be able to use you and VSO will help.

Volunteers are guaranteed an allowance based on local rates of pay. They get free accommodation, life insurance and health care. VSO gives them a grant for equipment and other necessities. And of course travel to and from the foreign land is free.

Even those who do not qualify as a volunteer overseas (perhaps because they are married with five children), can still join their local VSO group for information and for the chance to find out more about their neighbours overseas.

Useful addresses

British Refugee Council, Bondway House, 3–9 Bondway Street, London SW8 1SJ (tel 01–582 6922)

Catholic Fund for Overseas Development, 2 Garden Close, Stockwell Road. London SW9 9TY (tel 01–735 9041)

The Central Bureau for Educational Visits and Exchanges, Seymour Mews House, Seymour Mews, London W1H 9PE (tel 01–486 5101)

Christian Aid, PO Box 100, London SE1 7RT (tel 01–620 4444)

Christians Abroad, 11 Carteret Street, London SW1H 9DL (tel 01–222 2165)

Church of England Board for Social Responsibility, Church House, Great Smith Street, London SW1P 3NZ (tel 01–222 9011)

The Commonwealth Youth Exchange Council, 18 Fleet Street, London EC4Y 1AA (tel 01–353 3901)

Friends of the Earth, 26–28 Underwood Street, London N1 7JQ (tel 01–490 1555)

The Methodist World Affairs Secretary, 25 Marylebone Road, London NW1 5JR (tel 01–935 2541)

OXFAM, 274 Banbury Road, Oxford OX2 7DZ (tel 0865 56777)

Scottish Catholic International Aid Fund, 43 Greenhill Road, Rutherglen, Glasgow G7 2SW (tel 041–647 2113)

Tear Fund, 100 Church Road, Teddington, Middlesex TW11 8QE (tel 01–977 9144)
Voluntary Service Overseas, 9 Belgrave Square, London SW1X 8PW (tel 01–235 5191)
War on Want, Three Castles House, 1 London Bridge Street, London SE1 9SG (tel 01–403 2266)

Questions and coursework

1 Name two diseases which affect and often kill children who are starving.
2 What natural disaster often leads to starvation?
3 Zambia can survive only by exporting ....
4 Brazil can survive only by exporting ....
5 A million babies are born every five days. Most of them are born to the world's ....
6 According to the first book in the Bible, God orders us to be fruitful and ....
7 When we poison our rivers and the air we breathe, this is known as ....
8 Families forced to leave their homes and flee for their lives are called ....
9 Who led the ancient Jews from Egypt to freedom?
10 Who wanted to kill Jesus when he was a baby?
11 Britain has one teacher for every 20 pupils. Bangladesh has one teacher for every .... pupils.
12 One group of people wanting to help the world's poor have formed the Catholic Fund for Overseas Development. Name another such organisation.
13 Who organised 'Band Aid'?
14 'Love the Lord your God with all your heart, with all your soul, with all your strength and with all your mind; and your neighbour as yourself.'
What is your understanding of these two rules of a Christian life?
15 Try to identify the needy in the Third World today and plot their home countries on a map of the world. What do they have in common?
16 During World War II, six million Jews and Gypsies were exterminated under the Hitler regime. It is said that this must never happen again, and yet every *year* over 15 million children die of hunger. Comment.

17 You are in charge of fund-raising at school. Describe where all the money is to go and write a speech supporting your decision, to be given to a school assembly.

18 Find out about your local VSO and write an account of its work and the problems encountered.

19 In your own words explain clearly what is meant by poverty.

20 The world's population is increasing at such a rate that by the end of this century it is thought that it will be double what it was in 1968.

(a) What are some of the main causes of this increase in population?

(b) What problems are caused by an increasing population?

(c) What steps need to be taken to deal with these problems?

21 What are the Brandt reports and what are their main conclusions?

22 Name and describe a developing nation.

23 Read the following passages and answer the questions.

> 'When I was hungry, you gave me food; when thirsty you gave me drink; when I was a stranger you took me into your home; when naked, you clothed me; when I was ill, you came to my help; when in prison, you visited me.'
>
> Then the righteous will reply, 'Lord, when was it we saw you hungry and fed you, or thirsty and gave you drink, a stranger and took you home, or naked and clothed you? When did we see you ill or in prison, and come to visit you?' And the king will answer, 'I tell you this: anything you did for one of my brothers here, however humble, you did for me'

(Matthew chapter 25, verses 35 to 40, New English Bible)

> 'In every human being in need we are confronted by Jesus Christ himself and if we deny him in this encounter we cannot belong to him.'

(Christian Aid Policy Statement)

(a) Name one other organisation (excluding Christian Aid) which tries to put Jesus's words into practice.

(b) Briefly, outline two other biblical passages and show how they refer to concern for people in need.

(c) Explain how the Policy Statement is put into practice by Christian Aid or by any other organisation you have studied.
(d) If you were collecting money for overseas aid, how would you answer someone who said, 'Charity begins at home'?

24 'God, then, is on the side of the poor, the suffering, the refugee, the starving and the cruelly treated. He requires us to be on their side too.' How can you be 'on their side'?

25 Write a speech advocating an increase in Britain's overseas aid.

26 'Is it really sensible to use our rivers as open pipes to the sea, rather than keeping fresh water and foul separate?' Find out if river pollution is happening in your neighbourhood. What is the Christian attitude to such practices?

27 'God saw all that he had made, and it was very good.' (Genesis chapter 1, verse 30, NEB) In the light of this statement, read the following statement:

> Dead lakes and dying forests have become a trademark of modern industrialised society. Air pollution from industries, power stations and vehicles has blended a deadly chemical cocktail in the atmosphere.
>
> (Bo Landin, Swedish biologist)

Comment from a Christian point of view, and suggest some remedies.

28 'How hard it is for those who have riches to enter into the kingdom of God!' (Mark chapter 10, verse 23)
(a) What did Jesus tell the rich man to do?
(b) Find out what work is being done in your area to help the people of the Third World.

29 The second Brandt report stated, 'Only as education spreads, as health programmes keep existing children alive, as families have secure incomes which do not depend on increasing their numbers, will incentives for large families disappear and population growth be kept within manageable bounds.' (*Common Crisis*, Pan Books, p79)
Comment on this view.

3 Crime and Punishment

Responsibility

'Good behaviour has nothing to fear from magistrates,' wrote St Paul. 'Only criminals have anything to fear. If you wish to live without being afraid of authority, live honestly, and authority may even honour you. The State is there to serve God for your benefit. If you break the law, however, you may well fear . . . for the authorities exist to serve God. They carry out God's revenge by punishing wrongdoers.' (Romans chapter 13, verses 3f)

St Paul, like the ancient Jews, believed that 'God gives a just return, if we obey all he has commanded us to do'. The Bible can even suggest that God sends natural disasters as a punishment for wrongdoing. 'All those disasters which the Lord pronounced against us have now happened to us,' says the book of Baruch. 'And yet we have not tried to win the favour of the Lord by each one of us renouncing the dictates of his own wicked heart; and so the Lord has watched for the right moment to bring disaster on us.' (Baruch chapter 2, verses 7 to 9)

We can see notions of God's desire for a law-abiding people developing in the Bible, from the day when Moses gave the Jews God's Ten Commandments until the time of St Paul's writings. The Ten Commandments paint a picture of a God who says, 'I punish the father's fault in the sons, the grandsons and the great grandsons of those who hate me; but I show kindness to thousands of those who love me and keep my commandments.' (Exodus chapter 20, verses 5f)

Sons punished for sins of fathers

Does this seem fair?

It is unfortunately often true that children and even grandchildren may suffer a great deal owing to a parent's or grandparent's bad behaviour. For example, a drunken father does not produce a happy home, and an unhappy home can mark a child for life. Again, if leaders of a community rule unwisely or selfishly, injustice thrives and the weak suffer.

But does it seem right to say that God is punishing that unhappy child or the suffering weak? The Bible soon ceased to preach this. In one lovely image, the prophet Ezekiel declared that it is absurd to insist that because a father has eaten sour grapes, his children's teeth should be set on edge.

The prophet Jeremiah made the same point: 'Each is to die for his own sin. Every man who eats unripe grapes is to have his own teeth set on edge.' (Jeremiah chapter 31, verse 30, NEB)

This was a great leap forward. In the past, wrote Morris Ginsberg, 'Often the family or the kindred was made to suffer with the offender . . . The declaration in *Ezekiel* that it was unjust that the children's teeth should be set on edge when the father had eaten sour grapes was a revolutionary advance on the earlier view that the sins of the fathers should be visited on the children.' (*On Justice in Society*, Penguin Books 1965, pp165f)

Christians thus inherited from the Jews the notion that we are each individually punished by God only for whatever is our own responsibility. As St Paul put it, 'Each of us will get what we deserve.' (2 Corinthians chapter 5, verse 10, NEB)

1 God the judge

The God worshipped by Jews and by Christians is thus a moral God.

The prophet Nahum wrote a poem about God as an avenger.

> God avenges, he is full of wrath,
> God takes vengeance on his foes,
> He stores up fury for his enemies.
> God is slow to anger but immense in power.
> Most surely God will not leave the guilty unpunished.

Here God is seen punishing the guilty. The Bible also sees God as protecting the innocent

> 'Woe to those who make evil laws,
> to those who issue the commands of tyrants,
> who refuse justice to the unfortunate
> and cheat the poor people of their rights,
> who make widows their prey

and rob the orphan.
What will you do on the day of punishment?'
(Isaiah chapter 10, verses 1 to 3, RSV)

Unfortunately, events did not always seem to work out in this way for the Jews. Then as now the wicked can prosper and the innocent suffer. The immense sufferings of the Jews led them more and more to think that since they could find no justice in this world, justice must be done in the next.

Jesus often spoke in this way. 'A good man draws good things from his store of goodness; a bad man draws bad things from his store of badness. So I tell you this, that for every malicious word men utter, they will answer on the judgment day,' he said. The wicked will receive eternal punishment; the good eternal life. (Matthew chapter 12, verses 35f, and chapter 25, verse 46, JB)

Eternal punishment

St Paul came to believe that Jesus himself would be judging men and women after death. He declared that 'the truth about all of us will be brought out in the law court of Christ.' (2 Corinthians chapter 5, verse 10, JB)

A summary

The Bible, then, sees God as the supreme ruler of the world, who has given us laws and expects us to obey them. These laws involve loving and caring for our neighbours, as well as worshipping God.

Those who are evil, God will punish. Those who are good, God will reward. At first it was hoped that this judgment would happen in this world. Eventually Christians and Jews started looking for God's justice in the next world, in 'eternal life'.

Justice in the next world

On earth, however, we are still required to act for God, punishing evildoers on his behalf and so protecting the weak and innocent as well as trying to bring about a juster world.

The aims of punishment

Punishment here on earth becomes not something inflicted by God, or a kind of natural result of wrongdoing or stupid behaviour (the way, say, anyone who drinks to excess becomes ill the following morning). Punishment is deliberately inflicted by other human beings because of some clear offence. It is deliberately made unpleasant. We also know that prison sentences almost always affect the criminal's family, especially if the prisoner is also the breadwinner.

If we believe that we have the right or duty to punish wrongdoers in this way, we need to ask what should be our aims in inflicting such punishment. As an English thinker named Jeremy Bentham observed, 'All punishment is a mischief.' He added that if it ought to be accepted at all, it should be allowed only 'in so far as it promises to exclude some greater evil'.

1 Punishment as deterrence

Two aims of punishment (both found in the Bible) that might fit in with Jeremy Bentham's rule are:

1 punishment to stop the offender committing another crime, and
2 to stop anyone else from wanting to imitate his or her evil ways.

One book in the Old Testament declares that executing offenders 'banishes evil' not only by removing the offender but also because 'all the people shall hear of it and be afraid and not act in the same way again.' (Deuteronomy chapter 17, verse 13)

This defence of punishment is called the theory of deterrence. To 'deter' someone from an evil action is to prevent them committing it because they fear the consequences.

Fear of crime's consequences

This seems at first an attractive viewpoint, but does it work? Does, for example, imposing severe penalties on football hooligans deter other would-be hooligans? Does banning drunken drivers stop others from drinking before driving if they think they won't be caught?

One danger in this view of punishment is that it pays little or no attention to the needs of the criminal who is now being punished. He or she is simply being used by society, not helped and possibly not treated fairly. Criminals can be used simply as a means of helping to keep other criminal elements of society in order, not as human beings in their own right.

Some people have found this acceptable. In the

nineteenth century the Reverend Sydney Smith said that 'when a man has been proved to have committed a crime, it is expedient that society should make use of that man for the diminution of crime: he belongs to them for that purpose.' Others think that is to debase a human being.

A second danger of the deterrence view of punishment is that it can lead to increasingly savage penalties, in the hope of frightening off other would-be offenders. Judges in our courts who hand out such extreme sentences often call them 'exemplary' penalties, since they aim more at being an example to others than a punishment for the offender.

Deterrence sometimes works

We know that the fear of punishment does prevent some would-be criminals from committing crimes. In 1944, for instance, the Germans who had conquered Denmark deported nearly all the Danish police, thus greatly easing the lives of Danish criminals, who no longer expected to be caught and punished.

Such crimes as theft and fraud increased enormously. Sexual crimes and murders did not. Presumably the latter two sorts of crime are carried out by persons whose passions or even mental abnormality prevent them from making calculations about whether or nor they will be caught or punished.

Those criminals who are able to make such calculations do obviously make them. Deterrence can work.

2 Punishment as retribution

Those who object to such sentences often describe their own principle as one of retribution. Retribution, they say, is a 'punishment that fits the crime'.

Punishment to fit the crime

They argue that it is unjust to impose on any criminals sentences that they have not deserved. Although it would be easy to deter car drivers who park illegally by hanging a few of them, this punishment would be unjust since in no way would it match the evil involved in illegal parking.

One way of trying to make the punishment fit the crime is to make it match completely. 'Anyone who strikes a man and so causes his death must die,' says the Old Testament. It goes on: 'If, when men come to blows, they hurt a woman who is pregnant and she suffers a miscarriage, though she does not die of it, the man responsible must pay the compensation demanded of him by the woman's master; he shall hand it over, after arbitration. But should she die, you shall give life for life, eye for eye, tooth for tooth, hand for hand, foot for foot, burn for burn, wound for wound, stroke for stroke.'

The theory of 'retribution' and the theory of 'deterrence' are here united. If you know that chopping off a man's hand will mean that your hand will be chopped off, or that injuring a pregnant woman will cost you compensation, you may well try to keep out of fights.

The Old Testament laws about this were also subtle. 'If men quarrel and one strikes the other a blow with stone or fist so that the man, though he does not die, must keep to his bed, the one who struck the blow . . . must compensate him for his enforced inactivity, and care for him until he is completely cured.'

You can see too how much the Jews felt that children should respect their parents by the following rules.

> Anyone who strikes his father or mother must die. Anyone who curses his father or mother must die.
>
> (Exodus chapter 21, verses 15 to 25)

Even owners of dangerous animals could be held responsible for the animals' vicious behaviour.

> When an ox gores a man or a woman to death, the ox must be stoned . . . and the owner of the ox shall not be liable. But if the ox has been in the habit of goring before, and if its owner was warned but has not kept it under control, then should this ox kill a man or woman the ox must be stoned and the owner put to death.
>
> (Exodus chapter 21, verses 28f, NEB)

An eye for an eye, a tooth for a tooth

'An eye for an eye, a tooth for a tooth' perfectly sums up the idea of punishment as retribution.

This idea still appeals to many of us. For instance, during World War II, as we have seen in chapter 1 of this book, vicious Nazis slaughtered millions of innocent people. After the war many of these bestial criminals escaped from Germany to live peaceful, sometimes prosperous years in foreign countries.

In Vienna a Jewish Nazi-hunter named Simon Wiesenthal set himself to tracking them down and bringing them to justice. His persistence discovered and helped to capture some of the worst criminals of the twentieth century.

In particular Jewish Nazi-hunters kidnapped Adolf Eichmann, who had been responsible for the merciless deaths of countless Jewish men, women and children. Eichmann was brought from his 'safe' refuge and put on trial in Jerusalem. He was sentenced to death and executed.

Some would argue that little good was done in executing Eichmann for the mass-murders he had committed many years before. Not a single one of his victims was brought back to life. But others would say that at last he had 'paid for' his crimes with his own life.

Public condemnation of crime

One of the greatest moral thinkers of all time, a German named Immanuel Kant, argued that such executions were absolutely necessary unless society decided to forget all about justice. Kant believed that unless murderers were executed, every other citizen was behaving as if justice didn't matter.

To make his point more forcibly, Immanuel Kant wrote:

> Even if the inhabitants of an island decided to separate and scatter over the rest of the world, they should first of all execute the last murderer in their prisons. In that way each person would meet with the fate his deeds deserved. The guilt of blood would not rest upon everyone else.

It may seem savage to chop off someone's hand if he or she has chopped off the hand of another person, as the theory of retribution demands. It probably seems even more savage to kill a man if he has murdered another human being (and we will look at this question later in this chapter). But, in the words of R S Downie, 'The retributive theory, which is often taken to be an expression of barbarism, in fact provides a safeguard against the inhumane sacrifice of the individual for the social good' — which, as we have seen, is the moral danger of the deterrence theory of punishment. (R S Downie *Roles and Values*, Methuen 1971, p165)

The retribution system of punishment doesn't allow society to inflict a savager penalty than the crime demands. The criminal is punished only for what he or she has done, and not to deter others from committing the same crime.

3 Imprisonment for protection

J S Mill on self-protection

We also restrain criminals not simply for punishment but for our own self-protection. A famous defender of individual liberty, John Stuart Mill, insisted that this was the one and only justifiable reason for locking anyone away. 'The sole end for which mankind are warranted, either individually or collectively, in interfering with the action of one of their own number, is self-protection,' he wrote.

Since imprisoning people against their will is an offence against them, Mill argued, only if they are likely to harm others is it acceptable. So much did John Stuart Mill prize liberty that he went so far as to insist on any man's or woman's right to harm themselves, without any interference from the law.

One modern philosopher, Ted Honderich, has commented on this.

> The solitary drunkard or drug addict, consenting homosexuals, pimps and their customers . . . anyone who commits an act of euthanasia or attempts to commit suicide — all these individuals and many others who offend against customary morality are assumed by Mill's opponents to be harming themselves or their agreeing partners.

Mill, as Ted Honderich observes, would agree. However, Honderich continues, Mill's opponents argue that to suppose that these acts only harm those who indulge in them is a mistake.

> The addict makes himself incapable of contributing to society and so harms us all. Also, others may be influenced by him and so become addicts.
>
> (*Punishment, The Supposed Justifications*, Penguin edition 1971, pp191f)

It is possible, then, to argue that we may imprison offenders not simply to protect the rest of society, but also for their own self-protection.

4 Reforming the criminal

By and large people are kept under control by the community at large, not by punishment. Our own standards of behaviour, partly given to us by our parents, perhaps also derived from our religion, make us behave decently. What society expects of us also counts. If we go into a pub and continually get drunk, soon we shall be no longer welcome. If we always push our way to the front of queues, eventually other people will start to complain.

When these social controls break down and people do commit crimes, we must try to find a way of changing the criminals, of reforming them and returning them to decent social life again. This is the theory of punishment as reform, sometimes known as rehabilitation.

Rehabilitation

The Bible actually sees God himself as punishing in order to reform the wicked. 'Happy indeed is the man whom God corrects,' argues the book of Job. 'For God who wounds is the one who also soothes the sore, and the hand that hurts is the hand that heals.' (Job chapter 5, verse 17, JB)

Solitary confinement

In the nineteenth century some humane Christians used to argue that this aim was best achieved by putting prisoners into solitary confinement. There they would have time to think about their evil ways and repent. In Europe some Catholic prison reformers were inspired to run their jails in this way since they knew that monks and nuns, confined in their monastery cells, could develop deep spiritual lives. So they put prisoners in similar cells, cared for by priests and chaplains, but cut off from others.

In Pennsylvania, USA, the Quakers set up similar prisons, with inmates living in separate cells, cut off from other prisoners and usually with only the Bible to read. The Pennsylvania system soon spread to Europe.

Although these systems seem cruel today (for solitary confinement is nowadays used as an especially severe punishment in prisons), they had at least two real merits. Criminals in close confinement together, far from improving their characters, often train each other in criminality, learning 'secrets of the trade' from each other. Secondly, to live alone in a cell may be far preferable to living in the overcrowded conditions of many present-day jails.

Probation

A totally contrary view — though still aimed at reforming the criminal — is that prisons themselves are quite the wrong place for bringing someone back into society. How do you teach men and women to be free by keeping them behind bars? This view is a part of the theory behind probation. Probation is an attempt to protect society from offenders while keeping them out of jail.

Six hundred years ago, if a local offender could find someone to offer a money bond, which would be forfeited if he or she committed the offence again, then often the courts waived a jail sentence. The person offering the bond was expected to keep a close eye on the would-be offender — naturally enough, since otherwise his money was likely to be lost. In this fashion a kind of probation was introduced in fourteenth-century Britain.

Soon the custom was applied to actual, and not just would-be criminals. A hundred years ago the courts were regularly assigning voluntary minders to supervise young offenders. A main rule was that these minders must not be related to the culprits. In 1876 the Church of England started its 'Police Court Mission', staffed by Christians willing to work in conjunction with the police in supervising and trying to reform the 'probationers'. So successful was this work that the British government in 1907 passed the Probation Offenders Act, for the first time providing for the payment of probation officers.

A young person on probation first of all has his or her sentence suspended — thus escaping jail. Instead, for a length of time similar to the suspended jail sentence, the probationers are required to report regularly to their probation officers; and any serious failure to keep to the terms of probation orders will put the young offenders into jail after all.

Next the probation officer — today usually highly skilled in techniques of counselling — sets about trying to change the bad habits of the offender.

Probation officers enlist, if they can, the help of the offender's family. Teachers and employers, local clergy and youth leaders may all be willing to help to make the young offender a law-abiding, contented and useful member of the community.

Parole

Parole, like probation, was first introduced in Britain for young offenders. It was then extended to adults in 1948. *Parole* comes from the French for 'word', here meaning 'word of honour'. Offenders released early from jail are thus 'on parole', that is 'on their word of honour' to behave as decent members of society.

As with those on probation, offenders on parole are supervised outside prison, or sometimes simply required to report periodically to the police. The difference from probationers is that offenders on parole have all partly completed their prison sentences. If they 'break their parole', either by committing another crime of by failing to report regularly to the police, then they are sent back to jail.

The success of both parole and probation depends a great deal on the criminal involved. Some offenders are mentally retarded. Others have severe behaviour problems that few psychiatrists or social workers can solve. Many are poorly educated, which — along with the stigma of having been in prison — makes it hard for them to find work, acceptance and a place in society.

Helping criminals to become decent members of society without keeping them behind bars is also the aim of what are sometimes called 'community service orders'.

Community service

Although British courts introduced community service orders only in 1973, the idea is an old one. In the Middle Ages, instead of making people pay for their crimes in jail, offenders were forced to clean the town canals.

Today, convicted offenders may be asked to do up to 240 hours *unpaid* work in the community — thus in a way paying for their crimes. If they fail to attend the approved workplace, then they can be sent to jail instead. Since the scheme started, the courts have made great use of it. In 1985 for instance, 38,000 offenders (including 8 per cent of those found guilty of serious crimes) were punished in this way.

The advantages are that the offender has the satisfaction of doing useful work. Also, he or she may well be working alongside people who are obviously benefiting from the work — often the handicapped, or old and elderly persons. Thirdly, supervised by probation officers, the offender is no longer confined to the company of other criminals. Offenders work with non-offender volunteers, with people who can help them back into a decent community life.

Reform in prison

Even inside prisons, reform and rehabilitation have often been seen as two of the aims. When the English ran a penal colony in the nineteenth century at Norfolk Island off the coast of Australia, its governor, Captain Alexander Maconochie, introduced a system of marks given for good behaviour which could actually reduce a prisoner's sentence. These ideas were taken up in America. Prisoners were to be given industrial training. Good conduct was rewarded. The prison system was regarded as a 'halfway house' between total restraint and the community outside. Prisoners who co-operated had their sentences reduced.

Borstals

In Britain the reform movement also resulted in the Borstal system for young offenders. Begun in 1908, the system involved small prison institutions, with trained staff who supervised no more than 50 or so offenders. Psychologists and psychiatrists were to be on hand to help the inmates. Instead of performing mindlessly boring jobs such as sewing mailbags, inmates were to be given vocational training.

Ideal prisons

Reformers have produced many proposals for an ideal prison which would protect society from the criminal while

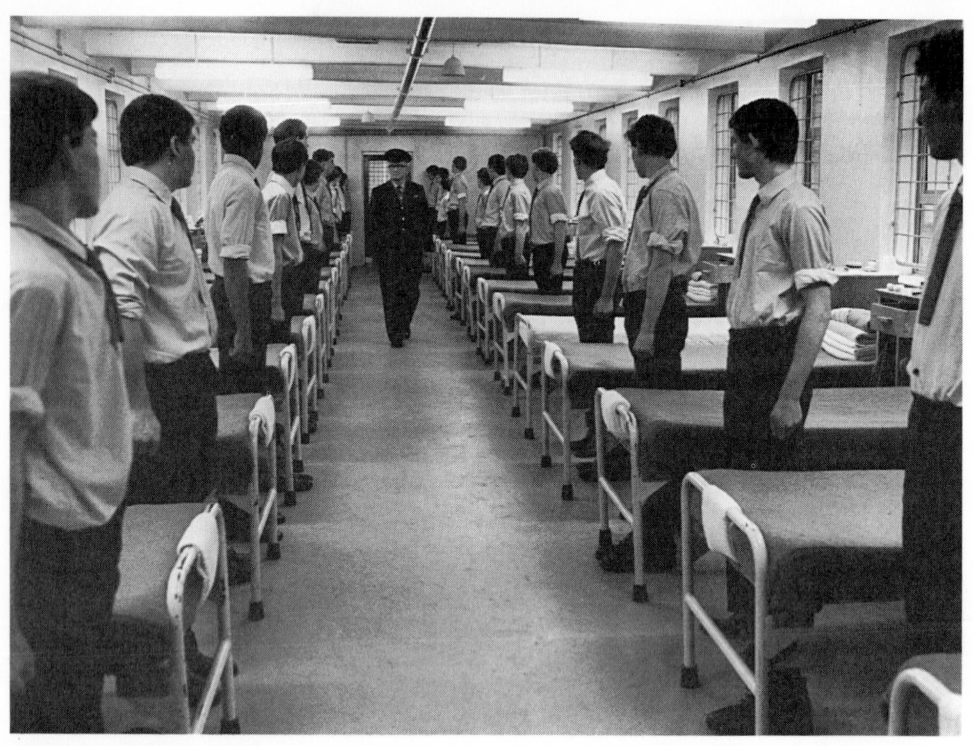

A detention centre for youths

refitting him or her for a decent life in the outside world. These ideas have rarely been completely put into practice, but they deserve thinking about. They include:

1 reducing sentences for good behaviour

Parole

Prisoners who have behaved well are sometimes let out on parole. One problem is that the prisoner can go through the motions of good behaviour, in order to gain early release, without really changing for the better.

2 responsible and rewarding work inside the jail

Training in prison

Again, such a policy will help to train a prisoner for living decently outside prison. Yet this policy has always proved difficult to put into practice. Sometimes prisons have been afraid to appear to be competing with the work of non-offenders — especially in times of high unemployment. In addition, prison staff are not always trained themselves in managing or supervising working prisoners. In any case, prison staff often have enough to do simply keeping their prisoners in order.

3 family visits

Keeping in touch

These do keep prisoners in touch with the outside world and the homes they hope one day to return to. But family visits in today's jails are often severely restricted. Sometimes a prisoner's family can speak to the inmate only through mesh or glass panels, often in the presence of other families doing the same, and almost always in the presence of guards or warders.

Also, lack of visiting facilities usually means that prisoners are lucky if they are allowed one short weekly visit from one family friend. Again, the imprisonment of a breadwinner can produce enormous hardship for the family, and many families cannot raise the cash for visiting, especially if the jail is far away. Finally, very few prisons allow space for sexual relations to take place between a couple, one of whom is a prisoner.

In short, family visits, though not despised by prisoners, scarcely keep them properly in touch with the outside world they hope one day to rejoin.

4 democratic rule inside prison

Most of us as adults expect some say in our own lives. We decide who we want to write to, and nobody else reads our letters. We expect either to have or to be given the right to vote. We can put ourselves up for Parliament or the local council. We decide when to go to bed. We can choose if we wish to organise a local football team or join a tennis club.

Giving prisoners a say

If people in prison have such rights taken away, how can the prisons be said to be training offenders for their eventual return to normal society?

Some prisons and reformatories have attempted to offer a measure of democratic control over prison life to the prisoners themselves. This makes further sense in view of the fact that prisons cannot be run without the co-operation of the prisoners themselves. But what tends to happen is not democratic control but the use of a few 'trusties' to control the rest of the inmates. Trusties get special concessions from the prison staff — extra comforts and privileges. They may often be tempted to use their special position to exploit the other prisoners.

5 work release

A new niche

Especially as prisoners approach the end of their time in jail, they need the chance to find a new niche in society. To throw a man out of jail without the prospects of work is to

Inmates working on the farm of an open prison

encourage him to turn back to crime. If a person's sole successes in life have consisted in stealing the goods of his or her neighbours, that person is unlikely to want to change these criminal habits for a workless life on the breadline.

Some prison systems therefore return men and women to society to work (or to look for work) as their term of imprisonment nears its end. Others even allow the inmates to leave the jail regularly during the term of imprisonment, in order to work outside.

6 education

In theory, all our prisons are meant to offer educational facilities to their inmates. Young offenders should not be deprived of their schooling. Older ones should have access to libraries, correspondence courses and the like.

The chance to catch up on schooling

In practice lack of staff and proper facilities makes this ideal more of a dream than a reality. And since many prisoners have in any case had problems with schooling and education, the poor quality of teaching inside the prisons is not much help.

What are criminals like?

The truth is we don't really know. The only criminals we can talk about are those who get caught. Apart from these, we can analyse crimes known to the police — again a limited sample, since many crimes (such as big-city fraud) are rarely detected.

Crimes of violence

A survey in America in 1962 revealed that thefts (of cars, and property worth more than $50) and burglary were seven times more frequent than crimes of violence (such as murder, rape and assault). In England and Wales in 1985 only three crimes in a hundred involved violence.

Further surveys have shown that people are more inclined to commit crimes at certain ages and that, leaving aside juveniles, people are at their most criminal between the ages of 20 and 24. Remember again that we are speaking only of those who are *caught*. (The statistics rarely include 'respectable' office workers who steal company paper or use company telephones for their private calls; even though clearly this too is theft.)

Women

Women commit far fewer crimes than men, save where prostitution and commercial vice are criminal offences.

Criminals who get caught

The great majority of criminals who end up in the courts come from classes of people with low incomes and poor, frequently changed jobs. Many too are under-educated and not very bright. These characteristics may well help them to fall into the hands of the police more easily than richer, brighter criminals. So it may be that the more powerful and intelligent classes in our society produce quite as many criminals as the rest; only they tend to get away with it.

1 Juvenile delinquents

Juvenile delinquents complicate the scene. Boys and girls who indulge in petty theft tend to reach a peak of delinquent activity around the age of 14. When it comes to more serious crimes, such as assaulting the police, stealing motor cars and committing malicious damage, juvenile delinquency peaks around 16 and 17. The great majority of these offenders are male; and the great majority settle down to law-abiding at the age of 22 or so.

What causes this juvenile delinquency? There are many suggestions: the emotional turmoil of teenagers; failure at school, leading to truancy and resentment; lack of cash, combined with a desire for status symbols such as a car, or at least an occasional joy-ride; the need to defy authority as teenage boys grow up; problems at home.

What ends this juvenile delinquency? Again, there are many suggestions: being caught and deciding to avoid trouble in future; marriage, children and one's own home; maturity; the benefits and responsibilities that come from the possibility of earning a living.

Inadequate homes

It has been shown that young people are more likely to behave in delinquent ways if their family life has been inadequate — especially if there is violence in the home, if their parents' discipline is too savage and if they feel unwanted. The young persons can respond by taking out their frustrations on society. And their feelings can persist for a lifetime.

The researcher Tony Parker met in prison a 30-year-old Irish alcoholic, who told him:

> I can't explain it properly: you know you've been robbed of something and as soon as you were born you were an embarrassment and a nuisance. I hate everybody, that's the fact of it; and most of all I hate myself.
>
> (Tony Parker *The Frying Pan*, Hutchinson 1970)

2 What are prisoners like?

From all this we can predict those more likely to end in jail and those likely to escape prosecution even if they are criminals. The less well educated, the retarded, those from poor homes and low-income groups are far more likely to suffer punishment than criminal groups from the rest of society.

Since they are poor, they are also likely to be unable to pay fines and so find themselves jailed instead. In 1985 24,000 people in Britain went to jail for not paying fines. Of these, 70 per cent were unemployed.

Finally, many of them will have been brought up in inadequate, violent homes.

What are prisons like?

British prisons are, by common consent, totally inadequate for our prison population. In June 1987 over 50,000 people were in custody in England and Wales, at a time when the

Violent protest resulting from inadequate conditions

Overcrowding

government's estimate of the normal prison accommodation was 41,603. In consequence our prisons are more crowded than they have ever been.

Lack of staff

Prison cells were designed for one prisoner. Over 13,000 prisoners are today living two to a cell, and over 5,000 three to a cell. Because of staff shortages some prisoners are kept locked up for 23 hours a day.

Prison officers too are suffering, for the prison environment is their working world. Most prisons are desperately insanitary. In 1985 22,000 of our prison cells had no access to sanitation. As a result around 26,000 prisoners were engaged each day in 'slopping out'.

Here is how the 1984 report of Her Majesty's Chief Inspector describes 'slopping out'.

> When the time for slopping out comes the prisoners queue up with their pots for the few toilets on the landing. The stench of urine and excrement pervades the prison. So awful is this procedure that many prisoners become constipated — others prefer to use their pants, hurling them and their contents out of the window when the morning comes.

Inadequate prisons

In such circumstances the high ideals of prison reformers and of prison officers who hope to do more for their charges than simply keep them locked up have little chance of success.

With prisoners crammed in cells and given little chance of reading or improving themselves in other ways, prisons are more likely to develop into schools for criminals. Prison violence is also more likely to break out under such conditions. Some heterosexual prisoners are more likely to be persuaded or forced to engage in homosexual acts.

1 Prison reformers

Jesus proclaimed that he had come to help captives and the downtrodden. He once went into a synagogue and read the words of the prophet Isaiah which say that the spirit of God has sent the prophet 'to bring good news to the poor, to proclaim liberty to captives . . . and to set the downtrodden free'. Then Jesus said, 'This text is being fulfilled today even as you listen.' (Luke chapter 4, verses 16 to 20, JB)

Inspired by him, individual Christians have often worked (sometimes in the face of great opposition) to improve the lives of those in prison.

John Howard

John Howard, for instance, who died in 1790, became High Sheriff of Bedfordshire. In the course of his duties he inspected Bedford Jail and was horrified by the prisoners' conditions. From that moment be worked to improve the sanitation of England's jail. He also insisted that the system of paying warders with fees from the prisoners themselves was absurd and that the warders ought to be paid wages instead.

Elizabeth Fry

Elizabeth Fry was another great prison reformer, a Quaker who lived from 1780 to 1845. Visiting Newgate Jail, London, in 1813, she was appalled at the plight of women prisoners. She set about improving their lot — tirelessly campaigning not only throughout Britain but in Europe too. Her aims included:

- separating imprisoned women from male prisoners;
- making sure that women prisoners were properly fed;
- insisting that women staff supervise women prisoners;
- seeing that the women in jail were suitably clothed;
- campaigning for light work for all women in prison.

2 Modern pressure groups

Today prisoners themselves have begun to press for reform and set up self-help pressure groups. PROP, an ex-prisoners' organisation was set up in 1972. As well as helping prisoners and their families, PROP provides medical and legal advice when prisoners complain about their treatment.

The APEX Trust was set up to help ex-prisoners trying to find work, offering them training in new skills and counselling. There is also NACRO, an organisation which aims to re-educate ex-prisoners and help them to find homes.

Other organisations care for women prisoners and ex-prisoners. Women Prisoners' Resource Centre visits every women's prison in Britain and helps women ex-prisoners returning to London to find homes. Women in Prison supports women ex-prisoners and crusades for improvements in women's prisons. Black Female Prisoners' Scheme specifically concerns itself with the needs of black women, both in prison and after their release, specialising in problems such as deportation, benefits and housing.

One organisation devotes itself to the whole question of a humane criminal justice system, namely the Howard League for Penal Reform, named after the great John Howard himself. And Radical Alternatives to Prison is a pressure group aiming at the total abolition of imprisonment.

The Howard League for Penal Reform

Capital punishment

As we have seen, the Old Testament decrees the death penalty for certain crimes, above all for murder. 'He who sheds man's blood shall have his blood shed by man.' (Genesis chapter 9, verse 6, JB). Yet almost all modern reformers and very many Christians believe in its abolition.

They could appeal for support to St Paul, who wrote:

> Bless those who persecute you; never curse them, bless them . . . Never repay evil for evil but let everyone see that you are interested only in the highest ideals. Do all you can to live at peace with everyone. Never try to get revenge: leave that, my friends, to God's anger. As

> scripture says, 'Vengeance is mine — I will pay them back,' the Lord promises. But there is more: 'If your enemy is hungry, you should give him food, and if he is thirsty, let him drink. Thus you heap red-hot coals on his head.' Resist evil and conquer it with good.
>
> (Romans chapter 12, verses 14 to 21)

Is killing someone because he or she has killed another human being repaying evil with evil?

1 The case for capital punishment

In many countries capital punishment is still allowed by law. Those who support it claim:

- it is a *deterrent* to other would-be murderers; and
- if carried out properly, it is fairly painless.

2 The case against capital punishment

The opponents of capital punishment point to considerable evidence that it cannot be proved to deter other would-be murderers.

In some countries the number of murders actually fell after it had been abolished. For instance, Canada got rid of capital punishment in 1976. The previous year 701 Canadians had been killed by their fellow men. In 1984 the number of persons killed by others had fallen to 668.

Why does the death penalty fail to deter (whereas other deterrents do have effects on crime rates)? The answer is quite simply that most murders and manslaughters are carried out by people unable to control themselves rationally. Sixty per cent of murderers are mentally abnormal or acted with diminished responsibility when they killed.

Its cruelty

Hanging, stoning, the gas chamber, electrocution, beheading, strangling and lethal injections are various ways in which states put those judged guilty of murder to death. Not one of these methods is clearly painless. Hanging violently jerks the victim's neck. Death by lethal gas can take up to eight minutes. Electrocution always produces the smell of burning flesh. Beheading, stoning and strangulation are savage. Lethal injections require doctors to search for a suitable vein in the arm of an often struggling victim.

Although prison guards and the head prison chaplain were convinced that he was innocent, Edward Johnson, pictured here during a final meeting with his grandmother 14 days before he died, was executed in Mississippi in 1987.

All this leaves aside the mental torment of a man or woman waiting, months or even years, to be judiciously put to death. Such cruelty, opponents of capital punishment believe, is unacceptable in civilised societies.

As Baroness Wootton wrote in 1969:

It degrades societies which carry it out

Immoral actions are generally degrading to those who perform them, or in whose name they are performed; and that is most conspicuously true of judicial execution. The whole monstrous ritual, the solicitous care for the condemned man's last days, the elaborate precautions taken to prevent him from taking his own life (why shouldn't he?), the stealthy introduction of the hangman into the prison the day before an execution, in order that he may surreptitiously observe his victim's physique from which to make the calculations necessary for the successful performance of his hideous task — what civilised man or woman could participate in all this wihout a sense of degradation?'

(quoted in *The Case Against Capital Punishment*, The Howard League for Penal Reform, p 9)

As Lord Chancellor Goddard put it during the debates that ended capital punishment in Britain, referring to earlier decisions to abolish hanging, disembowelling and quartering traitors, 'We did not abolish that punishment because we sympathized with traitors, but because we took the view that it was a punishment no longer consistent with our self-respect.'

Miscarriages of justice

Capital punishment is irrevocable. Once society has killed a man or a woman convicted of murder, there can be no going back. Yet innocent persons have been executed, in this century and in our own country.

A clear case is that of Timothy Evans, hanged in 1950 for alleged murder. In 1966 John Christie, the main prosecution witness at his trial, was himself convicted of a whole series of murders. The British Crown admitted its mistake. Timothy Evans was granted a posthumous pardon. It did not bring him back to life.

Since hanging was abolished in Britain, Patrick Meehan, Albert Taylor and John Preece were all found guilty of murder and (on later evidence) had their convictions quashed. But for the abolition of the death penalty, all three would now be dead.

3 Mercy and forgiveness

As well as upholding the right to punish crimes, the Bible also increasingly stresses mercy and forgiveness. 'As I live, says the Lord God, I swear I take no pleasure in the death of a wicked man but rather in the wicked man's conversion, that he may live,' wrote the prophet Ezekiel. (Ezekiel chapter 33, verse 11, RSV)

Jesus carried this teaching about mercy still further. Once he was asked whether a woman caught committing adultery should be stoned to death. He replied, 'If there is one of you who has not sinned, let him be the first to throw a stone at her.' When everyone else had slunk away, he asked the woman, 'Where are they? Has no one condemned you?' 'No sir,' she replied. 'Neither do I condemn you,' said Jesus. 'Go away and sin no more.' (John chapter 8, verses 3 to 11)

Jesus on forgiveness

Even as he himself was being put to death, flanked by two convicted thieves also being executed, one of them admitted to his fellow thief that whereas Jesus had done no wrong, 'We are paying for what we did'. He said to Jesus, 'Remember me when you come into your kingdom.' Jesus replied, 'Indeed, I promise you, today you will be with me in paradise.' (Luke chapter 23, verses 39 to 43, JB)

Useful addresses

The APEX Trust, Brixton Hill Place, London SW2 1HJ (tel 01–671 7633)
Black Female Prisoners' Scheme, Brixton Enterprise Centre, 444 Brixton Road, London SW9 (tel 01–733 5520)
Central Office of Information, Hercules Road, London SE1 (tel 01– 928 2345)
Howard League for Penal Reform, 320–22 Kennington Park Road, London SE11 4PP (tel 01–735 3317)
NACRO, 169 Clapham Road, London SW9 0PU (tel 01–582 6511)
PROP, BM-PROP, London W1N 3XX (tel 01–542 3744)
Radical Alternatives to Prison, BCM Box 4842, London WC1N 3XX
Women in Prison, 25 Horsell Road, London N5 1XL (tel 01–609 7463)
Women Prisoners' Resource Centre, Room a, 1 Thorpe Close, Ladbroke Grove, London W10 5XL (tel 01–968 3121)

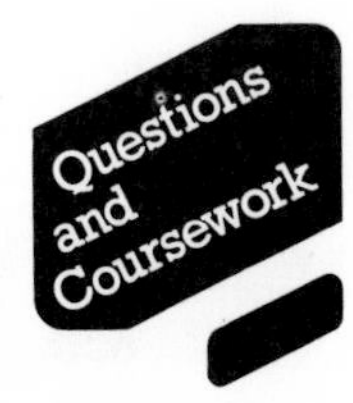

Questions and coursework

1 St Paul wrote that good behaviour has nothing to fear from ....
2 The Bible describes God as one who punishes the ....
3 'Those who are evil God will ....; those who are good God will ....'
4 Punishment that fits the crime is called ....
5 The Old Testament says that 'anyone who strikes a man and so causes his death must ....'.
6 In the Old Testament we are given the rule 'An eye for an eye and a .... for a ....'.
7 We restrain criminals not simply for punishment but also for our own ....
8 Complete the following saying: 'The hand that hurts is the hand that ....'.

9 .... is an attempt to protect society from people who have committed a crime, while still keeping them out of jail.
10 When a person has committed a crime, he or she can be made to clean out canals as a sentence. We call this ....
11 Jeremy Bentham observed, 'all punishment is a mischief'. What is your understanding of this statement?
12 Give reasons why we punish people, and comment on these reasons. Should 'the punishment fit the crime'?
13 Discuss the problems caused by putting people in prison.
14 Look at some ideas for criminal reform, commenting on them from a Christian standpoint.
15 List some of the reasons why people commit crimes.
16 Give some of the schemes and methods used to keep people out of prison.
17 Jesus proclaimed that he had come to help captives and the downtrodden. How would you set about improving the lives of those in prison?
18 Write an account of some of the groups who try to help prisoners.
19 You have to speak in a debate, opposing capital punishment. Write out your speech, including supporting evidence from the Bible.
20 Give arguments for and against the use of prisons as a means of dealing with law-breakers.
21 Which law would you like to abolish and why would you do so?
22 What do you know about Elizabeth Fry?
23 Describe some of the ways in which people break the law and say which of them you think are serious offences and why.
24 Do you think it is ever permissible for people to avoid paying taxes?
25 Can you justify using a company phone for private calls?
26 What do you know about detention centres?

4 War, Peace and Violence

Jesus's teaching

Blessed are the peacemakers

'Blessed are the peacemakers,' said Jesus. 'They shall be called the children of God.'

He continued:

> You have learned how it was said, 'Eye for eye and tooth for tooth'. But I say this to you: offer the wicked man no resistance. On the contrary, if anyone hits you on the right cheek, offer him the other as well; if a man takes you to law and would have your tunic, let him have your cloak as well. So if anyone orders you to go one mile, go two miles with him . . .
>
> You have learned how it was said, 'You must love your neighbour and hate your enemy'. But I say this to you: love your enemies and pray for those who persecute you.
>
> (Matthew chapter 5, verses 9 and 38 to 43, JB)

Jesus also ordered his followers, 'Do good to them that hate you.' (Luke chapter 6, verse 27, JB) When St Peter took out his sword to save Jesus from his enemies, Jesus stopped him using it, with the words 'all who draw the sword will die by the sword' (Matthew chapter 26, verse 52, JB).

Some Christians have understood these passages to mean that Jesus wanted to outlaw war and violence altogether. But the question is not so simple once you begin to look at other things he did and said.

Other evidence

The following episode shows that he was not totally opposed to violence.

> Just before the Jewish Passover Jesus went up to Jerusalem, and in the Temple he found people selling sheep and pigeons, and the money changers sitting at their counters there. Making a whip out of some cord, he

drove them all out of the Temple, cattle and sheep as well, scattered the money changers' coins, knocked their tables over and said to the pigeon-sellers, 'Take all this out of here and stop turning my Father's house into a market.'
(John chapter 2, verses 13 to 17, JB)

Jesus also met and praised soldiers whose lives and faith deserved it. Never do we find him telling them to give up their jobs. And something he said at his trial indicates that his words about turning your cheek to those who wish to hit you apply to individual Christians, not to the way society should protect its members from aggression. Jesus said, 'Mine is not a kingdom of this world. If my kingdom were of this world, my men would have fought to prevent my being surrendered to the Jews. But my kingdom is not of this kind.' (John chapter 18, verse 36, JB)

On this evidence the rules of Christian non-violence do not prevent states and their rulers from taking up arms in self-defence.

Later Christians

Some leading thinkers of the early church did not agree. A theologian named Tertullian, for example, asked how Christians could take up the sword when Jesus had declared that those who did so would die by the sword. 'How can Christians wage war,' he continued, 'or even become soldiers in peace-time, without the sword which our Lord has taken away?'

Others disagreed with this view. The Reformer Martin Luther in the sixteenth century was well aware of the two strands in Jesus's teaching — one preaching non-violence in the Christian realm, the other allowing the need for defence in this unjust world.

Martin Luther

Martin Luther was once asked whether he would exercise the right of self-defence if he was attacked by robbers. 'Yes, certainly,' he answered. 'I should wield the sword, acting like a civil ruler myself, since there would be no-one else about to protect me. I should fight for all I was worth and then go to the Holy Communion feeling that I had done a good work. But if I were attacked as a preacher, because of the Gospel, I would fold my arms and say. "Now, my Lord

Christ, here I am. I have preached about you; if my time has come I now commit myself into your hands." And then I would die.'

Martin Luther also pointed out that in his view Christians have a duty to protect others who cannot protect themselves, even if this means resorting to violence. 'For yourself, you are simply a Christian,' he declared; 'but when it comes to caring for your servant, you are a different person. Your duty is to protect him.'

The just war

So, for the most part Christians set themselves not to denouncing war but to deciding what could be considered a just war and what could not.

St Augustine

St Augustine (who lived from 354 to 430) argued that to wage war is only acceptable if it is fought to restore or defend the peace all men and women need to live with justice and harmony. Yet, he held, war was so destructive that it should be entered into only when every possible attempt to keep the peace and restore justice had failed.

Since individuals waging war indiscriminately on their own behalf were likely to produce far more evil than good, Augustine also maintained that a war should be waged only by proper authorities. He added a third rule: that the intention of those declaring war must be purely the hope of restoring peace and justice, and never selfish gain.

1 The seven rules of a just war

Eventually Christians worked out seven rules for deciding that a war was just. These are:

1 the war must be fought by a proper authority;
2 the war must be fought only as a last resort;
3 the war must be fought in a just cause;
4 the war must be fought with right intent;
5 the war must be fought with a reasonable chance of success;
6 the war must be fought to ensure a better future than could be hoped for without a war;
7 the war must be fought by just means.

Rule 1

Rule 1 means that individuals are not justified in making wars without the agreement of a properly set-up authority. It has the advantage of stopping mindless aggression. In today's world it means that only governments should declare and wage wars.

But this rule raises some problems too. One is in the case of a war fought by a people seeking freedom from unjust tyranny. Wars of liberation from conquerors have always been like this. Obviously the conquering power is not going to sanction a war against itself. But there is no other legitimate authority in the state. According to the traditional rules, rebels seeking freedom cannot wage a just war.

Rule 2

Rule 2 is much easier to defend. Before any war is contemplated every single effort must have been made to achieve its aims by less violent ways. Negotiations, appeals to international organisations, political heads of states urgently keeping in touch with each other in spite of extreme provocations — all these are vital.

Rule 3

What is the kind of 'just cause' referred to in rule 3? Many people would limit it to self-defence. Wars of aggression are no longer seen as a proper way of solving international conflicts.

However, states in the modern world often enter into defensive alliances with other states. When, for instance, Nazi Germany occupied Czechoslovakia in 1939, Britain and France, seeing that Hitler's next victim seemed likely to be Poland, guaranteed to support Poland. This agreement was signed on 25 August 1939. Hitler's troops invaded Poland on 1 September. On 3 September, Britain and France declared war on Germany, and World War II began.

However justified Britain and France were, their action was scarcely one of self-defence. The notion of a 'just cause' is not easily defined.

Rule 4

'Right intent' in rule 4 means that the aims of the war must be just. Once those aims have been achieved, it is hoped that the war can be speedily stopped. In fact, once wars start, passions can grow so heated on both sides that the victors often become unwilling to accept anything but the total surrender or destruction of their enemies.

Rules 5 and 6

Rules 5 and 6 clearly go together. Unless a nation fighting a just war actually wins it, the future will almost certainly be worse than if its people had simply accepted the injustice they were fighting against. Thousands — perhaps millions — will have been killed in a war that has solved nothing.

Rule 7

Finally, rule 7, the law of 'just means', is especially important. It implies that the war must be fought as far as possible sparing non-combatants and the innocent. Bombing hospitals and schools, cathedrals and churches, civilian homes and shelters is totally condemned by this rule. The rule also means that a war must be fought with extreme care that the degree of violence involved and the damage done will not be far worse than that suffered if the nation fighting a just war had not fought at all.

2 Realism about modern warfare

Reinhold Niebuhr

Has modern warfare made some of these demands impossible to fulfil? One American Christian, Reinhold Niebuhr, believed this had happened when it became possible to bomb one's enemy from the air.

In 1943, during World War II, Niebuhr declared:

> 'It is not possible to defeat a foe without causing innocent people to suffer with the guilty. It is not possible to engage in any act of collective opposition to collective evil without involving the innocent with the guilty. It is not possible to move in history without becoming tainted with guilt. Once bombing has been developed as an instrument of warfare, it is not possible to disavow its use without capitulating to the foe who refuses to disavow it.'
>
> ('The Bombing of Germany' in *Love and Justice*, ed D H Robertson, Meridian Books, Cleveland 1967, p222)

Reinhold Niebuhr believed that in cases where people had to go to war to defend the weak, they inevitably committed great evils. In his view, all that Christians in this position could do was hope God would forgive them.

But this did not mean that, in Niebuhr's view, *anything* can be forgiven in wartime. When in 1944 the British and Americans started 'obliteration bombing' of German cities, Niebuhr condemned them.

Why do men want to fight at all?

The question why people ever want to fight each other still needs to be asked. 'A powerful measure of aggressiveness has to be reckoned as part of man's instinctive endowment,' wrote the great psychiatrist Sigmund Freud after World War I. Man, he said, treats his fellow man like a wolf.

Aggression and the brain

We now know that there are regions of the brain which control or sometimes fail to control human aggressiveness. In 1920, for instance, there was a large outbreak of an illness known as 'encephalitis lethargica' which sadly damages the brains of children. Many of the children whose brains were so damaged turned out to be tremendously aggressive in later life.

In some animals too, scientists have established that certain areas of the brain, if tampered with, trigger off aggression. Animals, however, usually do not fight each other to the death. Only when hunting do animals tend to kill each other. When, say, dogs fight, the looser usually lies on its back, in its most vulnerable position. The winner then backs off. The squabble is over.

1 Men or animals

Unlike animals, human beings do fight to the death. We have been doing so in startlingly increasing numbers. For instance, during the Napoleonic wars (which lasted from 1790 to 1815) the average number killed per day was 233. During World War I (lasting from 1914 to 1918) it was 5,449. During World War II (lasting from 1939 to 1945) it was 7,738. And on 6 August 1945 a single atomic bomb dropped on Hiroshima by the Americans killed a staggering 80,000 (a total that by the end of the year had increased by another 60,000 deaths — all a direct result of that one bomb).

2 Weapons of war

This appalling increase can be partly explained by another striking difference between fighting human beings and fighting animals. Whereas animals use whatever weapons nature has endowed them with (tusks, antlers, teeth, claws), human beings create weapons. The increase in daily deaths from war over two centuries is undoubtedly due in part to the scientists who have improved the equipment we use for killing each other.

Refinement through the ages

Each generation has in fact come up with more refined ways of killing its fellow human beings. Sometimes the church has tried to outlaw the new weapons. The Lateran Council of 1139, for example, banned the use of the crossbow and the longbow. No armies abandoned them. To kill an enemy by means of the crossbow was far simpler than trying to pierce him with a spear.

It also meant that you never had to look your enemy in the eye, and thus risk seeing him as a fellow human being. In this respect our modern weapons make the act of killing even more impersonal. To drop napalm on peasants in a forest is infinitely less personal than, say, stabbing your enemy to death. But there have always been men prepared to do even this.

3 Three further points about war

Three aspects of modern warfare give a powerful impetus to this willingness to kill. One is that a war involves violence that has been given the blessing of authority, and soldiers are trained to obey the orders of those in authority.

Authority's blessing

Secondly, men apparently fight with lighter hearts because their country has sanctioned the war. Love of one's own people and one's own country is natural. Powerful feelings of patriotism make a soldier feel he is not fighting just for himself but for the nation. As Rupert Brooke put it in his poem 'The soldier':

Patriotism

> If I should die, think only this of me:
> That there's some corner of a foreign field
> That is for ever England.

Enemy is evil

Thirdly, during wars powerful propaganda machines operate to paint the enemy in the worst possible light. Allies, on the other hand, are presented in a completely different light. A curious example of this practice occurred in the case of Soviet Russia after she had allied with Britain and the United States against Hitler in World War II. The Soviet dictator Stalin was no longer seen for the brutal tyrant and mass-murderer that he was. People on the allies' side even began to refer to him affectionately as 'Uncle Joe'.

After the war was over and the so-called 'cold war' between the Russian bloc and the West began, the Russians were once again portrayed as evil communists seeking the overthrow of the capitalist world. Meanwhile the Russian propaganda machine set about depicting its former allies in the Western world as evil.

Once a soldier is given a picture of his enemy as somehow

less than human, or as some kind of savage, it becomes much easier for him to kill that enemy.

4 Human greed

Nations of course may go to war for unworthy reasons. Sheer selfish greed can be one reason. Wars are fought to take over the lands and wealth of others. Hitler's conquests, for example, were supported by the Germans partly because the Treaty of Versailles after World War I had taken from them valuable stretches of territory. But the attempt to set that right was swollen into an overmighty attempt to create a huge German empire, an attempt which in fact eventually exhausted the resources of the German people.

Some words of the New Testament are relevant here. 'Where do wars and battles between you first start?' asked St James. He continued: 'Isn't it precisely in the desires fighting inside your own selves? You want something and haven't got it; so you are prepared to kill. You have an ambition that you cannot satisfy; so you fight to get your way by force.' (James chapter 4, verses 1f, JB)

5 Human need

At the same time poverty and oppression sometimes make the poor of the world resort to violence as the only way they can see out of their troubles. As the first Brandt report put it in 1980, 'While hunger rules, peace cannot prevail. He who wants to ban war must also ban mass poverty.'

The arms trade

The arms trade, which springs directly from the warlike ways of the nations, helps to preserve mass poverty. Sixty-five per cent of the world's arms are sold not to the rich countries but to what we call the Third World. Britain, for example, exports four-fifths of all its arms to Third World countries, earning from this over twice as much as our government gives to those countries in overseas aid.

The profit motive

Yet more bizarrely, arms traders often serve both sides in a dangerous conflict. They do so quite simply for profit, leaving aside morality or straightforward wisdom. So, for instance, during the long Gulf War of the 1980s, Britain has supplied arms to both sides, to both Iran and Iraq.

Arms versus aid

The cost of spending huge amounts on arms means that far less is available to help the world's poor. World military expenditure in 1980 amounted to $450 billion. Two years later it had risen to $550 billion.

In the words of Cardinal Basil Hume, when he was lobbying the British parliament in 1985, 'The world community can continue to pursue the arms race, and build ever larger and more deadly weapons, or it can shift and move deliberately and urgently towards the provision of basic needs for our global family. It cannot do both. Either we invest in arms and death, or we invest in life and the future development of the peoples of the world.'

Arms or life

Cardinal Hume's statement represents a modern version of the vision of the Old Testament prophet Micah. Micah looked forward to a time when all nations would obey the will of God by living together in peace. Micah too knew that this involved caring for the earth, devoting resources to cultivating the land, ensuring that all shared its rich produce.

'God will wield authority over many peoples and arbitrate for mighty nations,' he wrote;

> they will hammer their swords into ploughshares,
> their spears into sickles.
> Nation will not lift sword against nation,
> there will be no more training for war.
> Each man will sit under his vine and his fig tree,
> with no one to trouble him.

(Micah chapter 4, verses 3f, JB)

Atomic bombs

During World War II (1939–1945) both sides used weapons capable of destroying cities in a way previously unknown. Dresden in Germany was almost totally obliterated and Coventry in Britain partly so.

The war against Japan was brought to an end in 1945 by yet greater destruction and death, the result of dropping two

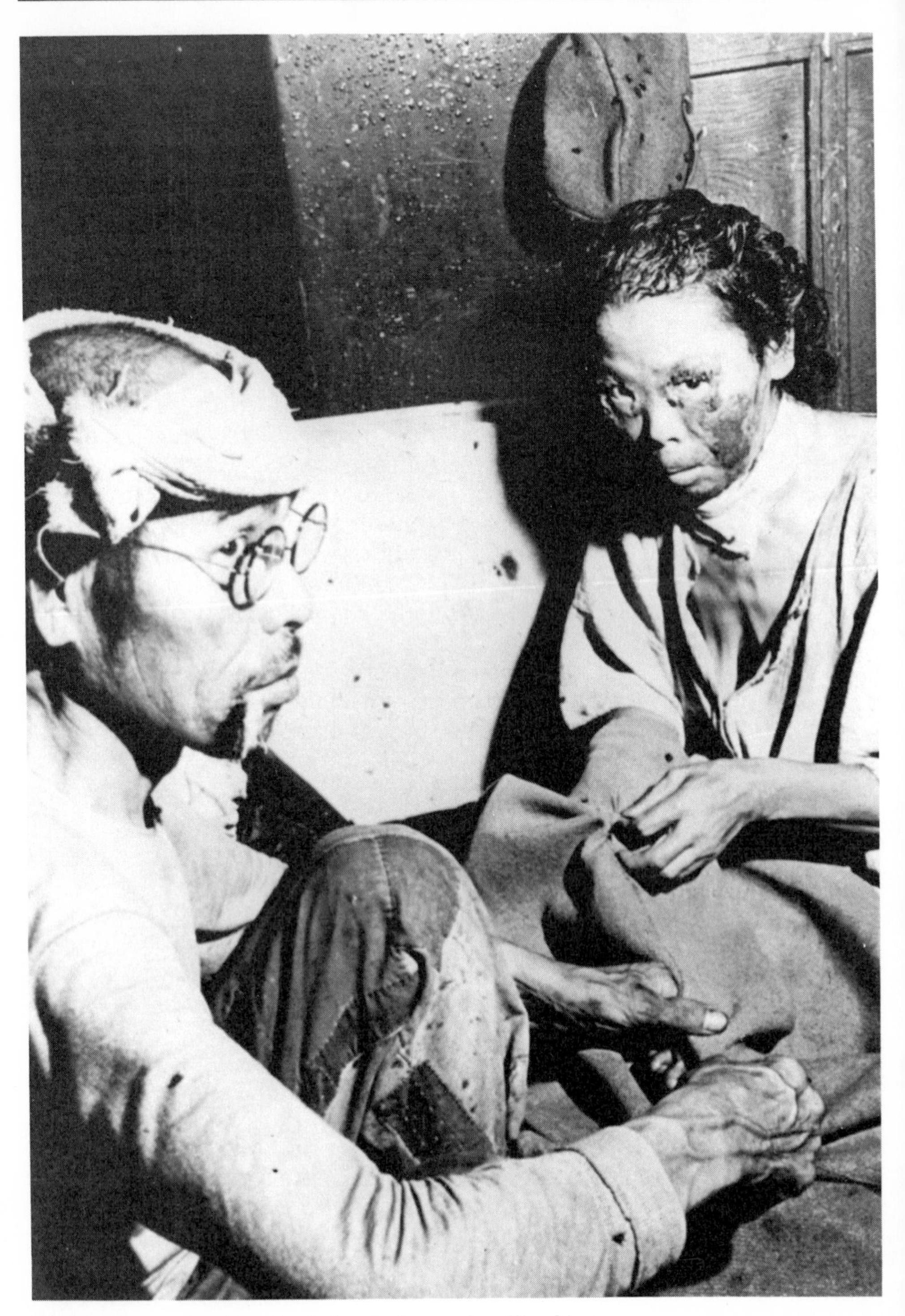

Victims who survived the atomic bomb dropped on Hiroshima

Hiroshima and Nagasaki

atomic bombs on the Japanese cities of Hiroshima and Nagasaki. The bombs on Hiroshima and Nagasaki are still killing people, through the long-term effects of radiation. The immediate effects were terrifying. The Japanese estimate that by December 1945 140,000 had died at Hiroshima and 70,000 at Nagasaki.

So far this has been the sole example of the use of nuclear weapons, but the nations have not ceased to develop such weapons. Today these are capable of unimaginable destruction.

1 The nuclear arms race

Only the United States of America and Britain possessed atomic bombs at the end of World War II. The Russians successfully exploded their first atomic bomb in 1949. The arms race had begun.

Both sides — Russia and the Western allies — developed even more devastating hydrogen bombs in the 1950s. The Americans and Russians took the lead in this arms race, but France, then China and soon other nations joined the superpowers and Britain in developing their own thermonuclear bombs.

Unknown effects

No one truly knows what would be the effect if the vastly superior weapons available today were ever used. Blast, fire and the radioactive fallout from a 20-megaton hydrogen bomb could easily destroy London. Its effects would then be uncontrollable by human beings, for huge amounts of radioactive matter would have been thrown up into space. Where this fell would then depend entirely on weather and winds. As in the case of the two much smaller atomic bombs on Japan, long-term effects of radiation would be terrible.

2 Deterrence

World leaders have responded to this appalling problem by turning to the idea of 'deterrence'. The theory of deterrence is simple: since everyone knows that all-out nuclear war would be suicidal, the arms race to keep up with the nuclear weapons of the enemy is carried on simply to frighten them. So long as everyone knows that in attacking another nation with nuclear weapons, fearful nuclear weapons would be unleashed in retaliation, then the world leaders will remain too terrified to use such weapons.

Balance of terror

Nuclear weapons are thus stockpiled not with the intention of using them but to create a so-called 'balance of terror'. A nuclear first-strike on another country by one of the great powers would result in partial or total destruction of the aggressor's own lands, cities and people, because the country attacked would instantly strike back.

Such a response is perfectly possible because no aggressor country today can knock out all the nuclear forces of its enemy, for these are protected underground in huge silos, hidden underwater in nuclear submarines, and ready for instant use in planes already in the air.

3 Problems

As defenders of the deterrence theory point out, there has in fact so far not been a nuclear attack since 1945. But frightening problems remain.

Whose advantage?

One is that enormous sums of money are being spent on nuclear weapons partly because no side dare allow the other to gain a possible advantage. There is always the fear that one country may succeed in outwitting another, producing a weapon that could win a nuclear war.

Limited war

Secondly, some military planners still believe that 'limited' nuclear wars could be fought. These would involve using smaller weapons with little radioactive fallout, and aiming them not at great cities but almost entirely at military targets.

Some military planners believe that if their country were attacked by a large number of non-nuclear forces, a limited nuclear response would soon stop the enemy, forcing its leaders to pause and even withdraw. At the same time military scientists are busy attempting to produce 'tactical' nuclear weapons, designed to be used only in war zones and against military targets.

Graduated deterrence

So these military thinkers have explored the notion of 'graduated deterrence'. The enemy would be held back first of all by smaller, limited weapons. If the enemy steps up the attack, maybe by using limited nuclear weapons itself, then the defenders' response will be to step up the nuclear arsenal. The idea of graduated deterrence would be at every stage to avoid bombing cities, aiming instead at military forces and military headquarters. Only as a last resort and in response to an attack on one's own great cities would all-out nuclear war occur.

4 Accidental nuclear war

Nuclear war could happen by accident. For instance on the morning of 3 June 1980 American air force officers monitoring the underground early-warning system in the Colorado Mountains were horrified to read on the display screens a warning that the Soviet Union had launched a nuclear attack on the United States from its land-based missiles and nuclear armed submarines. The displays indicated that these missiles would take fewer than 10 minutes to reach their targets.

False alarm

At an instant signal US crews of 116 B-52 nuclear bombers began to prepare for take-off. Nuclear submarine commanders were alerted. Launch keys were inserted to fire intercontinental ballistic missiles. At the last moment the scientists discovered that there was no Soviet attack on America. The early-warning system had suffered a computer error.

Accidental contamination

Nuclear contamination has already happened by accident, several times. One example occurred in 1966 when an American B-52 crashed near Palomares in Spain, dispersing radioactive plutonium to such an extent that the cost to the USA for cleaning up the contamination was $50 million. Far worse was the Chernobyl disaster of 1986, when vast amounts of radioactive matter spilled out of a Russian nuclear power station that was totally out of control.

Nuclear weapons and the just war

Some observers believe that a nuclear war between the superpowers would obliterate both sides, or substantial parts of their populations. No one could be said to 'win'. On this depends, as we have seen, the idea of deterrence: that the power subjected to a nuclear attack would deliberately obliterate most of its enemy's great cities.

But some people still believe that a nuclear war can be won: that, far from committing suicide, the stronger, better-equipped side could emerge with much of itself intact — even if, say, some 10 million persons died.

The seven rules

How far does this fit in with the traditional sevenfold Christian definition of a 'just war'?

Certainly a nuclear war might be fought in a **just cause**, with **right intent**, as a **last resort** and (if one combatant is much better equipped than the other) with a **reasonable chance of success**. And at present only **governments** can wage nuclear war, since no single individual possesses the means to do so.

Is it also possible to maintain that a nuclear war can be fought:

- with any possibility of sparing non-combatants?
- to ensure a better future than could be hoped for without a war?
- with the certainty that the degree of violence involved will not be far worse than what will happen if you don't fight at all?

Many would answer no to the last three questions. Nuclear warfare clearly threatens far more destruction and death than any good it might deliver.

1 A Christian response

Pope John Paul II, deeply concerned with this problem, ordered a study from Catholic scientists on the consequences of using nuclear weapons. One of its conclusions was:

> Recent talks about winning or even surviving a nuclear war must reflect a failure to appreciate a medical reality: Any nuclear war will inevitably cause death, disease and suffering of pandemonic proportions and without the possibility of effective medical intervention. That reality leads to the same conclusion physicians have reached for life-threatening epidemics throughout history: Prevention is essential for control.

A Christian vision

The second Vatican Council (a series of meetings of every Roman Catholic bishop, set up by the Pope in 1959) declared:

> As long as extravagant sums of money are poured into the development of new weapons, it is impossible to devote adequate aid in tackling the misery which prevails at the present day in the world. Instead of eradicating

British citizens demonstrate against nuclear arms

> international conflict once and for all, the contagion is spreading to other parts of the world. New approaches, based on reformed attitudes, will have to be chosen in order to remove this stumbling block, to free the earth from its pressing anxieties, and give back to the world a genuine peace.

Mutual disarmament

Pope John Paul II (in a message of 13 December 1981) insisted that the only logical step towards permanent peace is for countries to work for mutual disarmament. He said, 'I have in fact the deep conviction that, in the light of a nuclear war's effects, which can be scientifically foreseen as certain, the only choice that is morally and humanly valid is represented by the reduction of nuclear armaments, while awaiting their future complete elimination, carried out simultaneously by all parties, by means of explicit agreements and with the commitment of accepting effective controls.'

Many other Christians agree. Others go further, arguing for 'unilateral' disarmament. Their view is that since no one should contemplate ever using nuclear weapons, it is better for a country to give them up altogether even though, some would argue, this lays one open to nuclear threat from an enemy.

Pacifism

As we have seen, the refusal of many members of the early Christian church to take part in wars was short-lived. Instead Christians began to try to justify certain kinds of war while still condemning others.

But some men and women have always refused to do this. Those who condemn war totally — either each and every war, or particular ones — and refuse to fight even in self-defence are known as 'pacifists'.

Quakers

The group of Christians who have most consistently opposed war outright are those who belong to the Society of Friends, popularly known as 'Quakers'. Founded in Britain in the 1640s by a man named George Fox, in 1682 they took root also in Pennsylvania, USA, under the inspiration of William Penn.

Their absolute rejection of war is shared by other groups, notably Plymouth Brethren, Mennonites and

Christadelphians. Often men espousing such beliefs have been savagely punished by states on whose behalf they have refused to fight. At other times they have served in wars under great danger in such non-combatant roles as ambulance drivers.

Christian opposition

Pacifists take as central to Christianity the words of Jesus with which this chapter begins. Those who oppose their views have argued that these words simply do not apply to the politics of this world. Thus the American Protestant Reinhold Niebuhr once baldly declared that 'The ethical demands of Jesus are incapable of fulfilment in the present existence of man.'

Roman Catholicism has similarly traditionally taught that pacifism is wrong and just wars are morally acceptable. Pope Pius XII stated in 1953 that 'even today the right of any State to stand on the defensive cannot be denied.' But an increasing number of Catholics have argued that nuclear war is both so violent and so destructive that the rules of the just war no longer apply.

Non-violent protest

In our century two men, one an Indian, the other a black American, have been in the forefront of movements to bring about peaceful change by non-violent protest. Neither would live by the sword. Both of them were assassinated.

1 Gandhi

Mohandas Karamchand Gandhi, who is generally known as Mahatma (ie 'great soul') Gandhi, was born in west India in 1869. He studied law in England before moving to South Africa as legal champion of the Indian community there.

The Indians could, he taught, gain their proper rights simply by refusing to co-operate with the South African authorities. Already he was developing principles of non-violent resistance (which he called in Sanskrit '*satyagraha*', a word meaning 'devotion to truth') that he was to develop and successfully use for the rest of his life.

'Non-violence is the law of our species,' wrote Gandhi, 'as violence is the law of the brute.' But his tactics were not without physical danger. In Durban in 1897 Gandhi was beaten and almost lynched by white thugs. He refused to prosecute them.

During his time in South Africa Gandhi himself was frequently thrown into jail. His followers too suffered, especially in 1913, when thousands of Indian men and women were threatened with floggings (some of which were inflicted), shooting and imprisonment. Hundreds in fact went to prison. But the effect was great. Both Britain and India put pressure on the South African whites to agree to a compromise which Gandhi himself had worked out with the South African politician Jan Christian Smuts.

Gandhi in India

Gandhi returned to India the following year. In 1919, when the British, who then ruled India, passed laws enabling the authorities to imprison without trial Indians they suspected of sedition, Gandhi proclaimed another non-violent response. The British in turn reacted violently. British soldiers for example killed nearly 400 Indians at a meeting held at Amritsar in the Punjab.

Gandhi's leadership of the *satyagraha* struggle had brought him to the fore of Indian politics. He took over the Indian National Congress, advocating a policy of non-cooperation with all British organisations in India — whether law courts, schools or offices. Sentenced to six years in jail, he served two (being released in 1924 after a serious operation).

Gandhi's leadership during his two years in prison had been seriously missed by the Indian National Congress party. During the years of non-cooperation between 1919 and 1920 members of the two great religions in India, Hindus and Moslems, had worked together in unity. Now they were at odds with each other. Gandhi announced that he would go on a fast, a personal sacrifice, to force them to act together again in the interests of non-violence.

The British must go

But his chief aim was to get the British out of India so that the Indians could rule their own country. The British responded by setting up a group to reform the Indian constitution. Not one member of the group was an Indian. The Indian National Congress party decided to have nothing to do with it. In 1928 Gandhi proposed a resolution at the Calcutta Congress threatening a nation-wide non-violent campaign unless the British granted India complete independence.

In 1930 he inspired a massive *satyagraha* protest against the unjust tax on salt — a tax which severely hurt the poor of

Gandhi protests against the salt-tax in 1930

India. The result was that the British jailed more than 60,000 Indians. And although Gandhi agreed to visit London to try to come to some reasonable agreement on transferring power, the following year the authorities jailed him again.

Untouchables and the poor

If they thought to keep him quiet, they were mistaken. The very lowest class in India were called 'Untouchables'. Most people despised them. Gandhi called them 'children of God'. In prison he began another fast, threatening to continue it to death unless the Untouchables were given new political rights.

World War II found Gandhi supporting Britain against Hitler while also demanding immediate self-government. Once again Britain reacted foolishly, by imprisoning him and all the National Congress leaders. Self-government could not be far away; but during Gandhi's enforced absence

Muslims and Hindus

Muslems and Hindus were again at odds. When the British government finally quit in 1947, India was divided into two parts, the Muslims being given a new dominion called Pakistan.

The result was a huge refugee problem, as people fled from areas of the country where they no longer felt they belonged. There was enormous violence, and countless riots. Gandhi fasted until the rioting ceased in Calcutta. He persuaded the people of Delhi to come together in peace.

Hindu fanatics hated someone of their own religion advocating friendship with Muslims. On 30 January 1948 this great apostle of non-violence, on his way to evening prayers, was shot dead by a Hindu named Nathuram Godse.

Gandhi's ideas

The impetus towards peace and non-violent protest was sown in Gandhi's mind by Quakers whom he met in South Africa. He remained a Hindu, though he insisted that all great religions had deep insights into truth. Only human limitations result in our misunderstanding these insights.

So Gandhi was willing to learn from different religions. From Hinduism he took the notion that inner peace enables a man or woman to suffer anything, caring neither for victory nor failure. From Christianity he took with total sincerity Jesus's words about turning the other cheek.

Tolstoy and Gandhi

He became fascinated by the writings of a great Russian pacifist, the novelist Count Leo Tolstoy.

Tolstoy in 1879 had become a passionate Christian of a most unusual kind, living (after a life of self-indulgence) as a

vegetarian, renouncing the great novels he had written, dressing as a peasant, giving his property away to various members of his family. Above all, under the influence of Jesus, Tolstoy preached total pacifism and non-violence.

Gandhi and Tolstoy wrote to each other. The young man learned from the older. And to this Russian Christian's views on non-violence Gandhi added the insights of another great world religion: Buddhism.

Gandhi and the Buddhist notion of ahisma

Buddhists over centuries had developed a notion called *ahisma*, which means 'non-injury'. According to this teaching, we need to develop inside ourselves not only the belief that injuring someone else is wrong. We must also try to destroy even the wish to harm another person.

Harming another, according to the principles of *ahisma*, includes even embarrassing them. Gandhi's non-violence, as a result, was designed never to provoke his opponents (though it very often did). His aim was to appeal to their own consciences.

Gandhi's success

Gandhi's successful use of non-violence thus depended partly on the fact that his British opponents in the end were forced to ask whether or not their own behaviour fitted their deepest moral views.

Gandhi could appeal to the conscience of the British, since they *claimed* to be running their empire on moral principles. In the words of a German Christian commentator:

> In spite of the questionable nature of British policies, the men in charge could not act as if ethical norms were non-existent. It is true that they could wink at what was going on, as happens in politics. It is true that they could even use ethical principles as a pretext for very different and highly egoistic manipulations. They could be guilty of hypocrisy, or else make no secret whatsoever of their sacred egoism ('my country, right or wrong'). All this was quite possible. What was not possible was that Gandhi's efforts should make no impression on a political power which at bottom acknowledges ethical principles. Such a government is bound to be embarrassed and stymied when its opponent sets it so continually and publicly in the wrong, simply by acting according to distinctly ethical maxims — and suffering.
>
> (Helmut Thielicke *Theological Ethics*, Vol II, tr W H Lazareth, A & C Black 1969, p517)

The question remains whether such tactics of non-violence as Gandhi advocated and practised would work against an opponent who didn't care at all about morality in politics.

2 Martin Luther King

Martin Luther King, the black Baptist minister who led the massive civil rights movement in America from the mid-1950s until he was shot dead by a white man named James Earl Ray on 4 April 1968, was deeply inspired by Gandhi's teachings on non-violence.

He knew that (as he put it) non-violence will not accomplish miracles overnight. 'Men are not easily moved from their mental ruts or purged of their prejudice and irrational feelings,' he pointed out. 'When the underprivileged demand freedom, the privileged at first react with bitterness and resistance.'

Youth and marriage

A brilliant scholar, born in 1929 in Atlanta into a family where both his father and grandfather on his mother's side were Baptist preachers, Martin Luther King achieved the highest university honours.

At Boston University he met Coretta Young, a music student at New England Conservatory, and soon they were married. She bore him four childen, and he became a Baptist minister in charge of a church in Montgomery, Alabama.

Blacks on buses

At that time black and white people were officially kept apart on Montgomery buses. On 1 December 1955 a woman named Rosa Parks refused to give up her seat on a public bus to a white passenger. She was arrested.

Martin Luther King set up the Montgomery Improvement Association to get the law changed. Blacks boycotted the transport system, and in just over a year the law had been changed.

National success

From then on King organised blacks throughout the South to take on the unjust laws which gave whites greater privileges and positions throughout America. His home was threatened, as were his family. He was unjustly imprisoned after protesting with 33 others against separate lunch counters for blacks and whites in an Atlanta store.

Police with dogs and hoses attacked him and his followers as they demonstrated. He was jailed again in Birmingham, Alabama, in 1963; but he was convinced that his tactics were

Martin Luther King leading the civil rights movement in America

right. 'We shall match your capacity to inflict suffering with our capacity to endure suffering,' he told his opponents.

Martin Luther King had visited India in 1959 and discussed *satyagraha* with some of Mahatma Gandhi's followers. But in one important respect his own philosophy of non-violence differed from Gandhi's.

Gandhi's views made him opposed even to embarrassing an enemy. King deliberately intended to provoke, though always non-violently.

Letter from Birmingham Jail

'Non-violent direct action seeks to create such a crisis and foster such a tension that a community which has constantly refused to negotiate is forced to confront the issue,' he wrote from Birmingham Jail. 'It seeks so to dramatize the issue that it can no longer be ignored.'

Black self-respect

King also knew that once the black men and women began to demand their rights in such a fashion, their own feelings of self-respect would be transformed. As he said, 'the non-violent approach does something to the hearts and souls of those committed to it. It gives them new self-respect. It calls up resources of strength and courage that they did not know they had.'

He was also deliberately appealing to the consciences of many white Americans. Over 250,000 people, black and white, joined him on a march to Washington in 1963. The peaceful demand for human rights resulted in the passing of the Civil Rights Act of 1964 and the Voting Rights Act of 1965.

A dream of peace

In 1964 Martin Luther King had been awarded the Nobel Peace Prize. He now found himself opposed by black activists who were preaching violence as the way to demand further rights. He refused to change his own ways. And he turned against the American involvement in the Vietnam war.

He once spoke about his dream 'that my four little children will one day live in a nation where they will not be judged by the colour of their skin but by the content of their character.'

In 1968 be planned a poor persons' march on Washington. But before that he decided to visit Memphis, Tennessee, to show his support for the city's sanitation workers, who were on strike. There he was assassinated. On the day before his death he had declared:

> I've been to the mountain top. And I've looked over, and I've seen the promised land. I may not get there with you, but I want you to know tonight that we as a people will get to the promised land. So I'm happy tonight. I'm not worried about anything. I'm not fearing any man. Mine eyes have seen the glory of the coming of the Lord.

Useful addresses

Campaign against Arms Trade, 11 Goodwin Street, London N4 3HQ (tel 01–281 0297)

Campaign for Nuclear Disarmament, 22 Underwood Street, London N1 7JG (tel 01-250 4010)

Families for Defence, 45 Bloomsbury Square, London WC1A 2RA (tel 01-831 0180)

Pax Christi, St Francis of Assisi Centre, Pottery Lane, London W11 4NQ (tel 01–727 4609)

Quaker Peace and Service, Friends House, Euston Road, London NW1 2BJ (tel 01–387 3601)

Questions and coursework

1. Jesus described peacemakers as the ....
.... :
2. Jesus taught people to 'love your ....'.
3. Which great Christian leader declared that if attacked by robbers he would defend himself with the sword?
4. Christians have worked out seven rules for deciding what is a .... war.
5. On 6 August 1945 an atomic bomb was dropped on the city of ....
6. According to the Brandt report of 1980, 'He who wants to ban war must also ban mass ....
7. World leaders do not lead their countries to attack other countries with nuclear weapons, because they are afraid of being similarly attacked in return. This way in which peace is preserved is known as ....
8. Name the place where a nuclear disaster occurred in 1986.
9. Those who totally condemn war and refuse to fight are called ....
10. What name was given to the very lowest class in India?
11. List the seven rules of a just war and express your thoughts about them.
12. What moral or personal problems are faced by religious people who are involved in supporting war as soldiers or civilians?
13. Some people think ordinary wars are all right, but would not accept a nuclear war. What religious reasons might they give for:
    (a) fighting an ordinary war;
    (b) not fighting a nuclear war?
14. What is the difference between unilateral disarmament and multilateral disarmament?
15. As a nation we spend a great deal on defence and arms. Give the reasons why a Christian might support the country's military spending. Give next the reasons why a Christian might oppose it.
16. Does the Bible have a common view on war?
17. 'Give us peace in our time, O Lord; because there is none other that fighteth for us, but only Thou, O God.'
    (a) Describe *three* conditions of life necessary for nations to live in peace with other countries.

(b) Is there a time when going to war can be justified? Give reasons for your answer.
(c) How can Christians use individual aggressive instincts for the common good? Explain your answer.

18 'Where do wars and battles between you first start?' asked St James. Make a list of the reasons why wars begin. Comment on them.
19 How far can you apply the rules of a just war to a nuclear war?
20 Give an account of one man in the twentieth century who tried to bring about peaceful change by non-violent protest.
21 'All Christians should be pacifists.' Discuss and give your own views on pacifism.
22 What are the Christian teachings relevant to the question of nuclear warfare?

5 The Family and the World Outside

Marriage

Jesus told his followers, 'In the beginning at the creation, God made them male and female. For this reason a man shall leave his father and mother, and be made one with his wife; and the two shall become one flesh. It follows that they are no longer two individuals: they are one flesh. What God has joined together, man must not separate.' (Mark chapter 10, verses 6 to 8, NEB)

One flesh

Jesus as a Jew is here drawing his inspiration from the first book of the Bible, where the creation of the world is described in splendid picture language. God, we are there told, created man and woman in his own image (Genesis chapter 1, verse 27). A few paragraphs later comes the legend of God creating woman out of the first man's rib. In this fine story, which we need not take for a scientific fact, the man rejoices at the creation of his partner, describing her as 'bone of my bones and flesh of my flesh.' So the Bible sets out in poetry the essential union between partners that creates a marriage, adding the words quoted by Jesus, that a man shall leave his father and mother to be united to his wife as one flesh. (Genesis chapter 2, verses 23f)

1 Love and respect in marriage

The New Testament makes it clear that the great virtues of love and respect are what make a marriage superb. Since a man and woman have become one flesh in a marriage, they must love each other with precisely the same love as they have for their own selves. Children too have their duties in a family, but they also have the right to a proper respect. Here is the Bible's recipe for marriage.

'Till death us do part': the joy of life-long marriage

> Men are bound to love their wives, as they love their own bodies. In loving his wife, a man loves his own self; for no-one ever hated his own body. On the contrary, he provides and cares for it

says the letter to the Ephesians.

> Each of you must love his wife as his very self; and the woman must see to it that she pays her husband every honour.
>
> Children, obey your parents, for it is right that you should. 'Honour your father and mother' is the first commandment with a promise attached, in the words: 'that it may be well with you and that you may live long in the land'.
>
> You fathers, again, must not goad your children to resentment, but give them the instructions, and the correction, which belong to a Christian upbringing.
>
> (Ephesians chapter 5, verses 28, 29 and 33; chapter 6, verses 1 to 4, NEB)

The early Christians lived in a society where women were generally regarded as inferior to men. Jesus's loving and courteous attitude to women began to change this, for he regarded them with deep respect, offering to some despised women much praise. As a result, we can see a new spirit emerging in the earliest Christian writings (those in the New Testament) when they describe marriage. The view is still frequently held that the proper role of a wife is to be submissive to her husband. But there is now a new spirit of respect for women. St Peter, himself married, believed that a Christian woman's love and affection were strong enough to convert her unbelieving husband. He describes his ideal of married life like this.

Jesus's respect for women

> You women must accept the authority of your husbands, so that if there are any of them who disbelieve the Gospel they may be won over, without a word being said, by observing the chaste and reverent behaviour of their wives. Your beauty should reside, not in outward adornment — the braiding of the hair, or jewellery, or dress — but in the inmost centre of your being, with its imperishable ornament, a gentle, quiet spirit, which is of high value in the sight of God. Thus it was among God's people in the days of old: the women who fixed their hopes on him adorned themselves by submission to the husbands.

Then St Peter continues by describing the true behaviour of a husband in response to such a wife.

> In the same way, you husbands must conduct your married life with understanding: pay honour to the woman's body, not only because it is weaker, but also because you share together in the grace of God which gives you life.
>
> (1 Peter chapter 3, verses 1 to 7, NEB)

2 A picture of marriage at its finest

The novelist D H Lawrence in his story *The Rainbow* describes the security and peace of heart that comes from a stable marriage: security for a husband named Brangwen, his wife, and his stepdaughter Anna. Brangwen works happily, absorbed, scarcely conscious of the strength of his marriage till he and his wife come together again at the end of each day. Whenever she needs him, she calls, and he likewise. In the great protective arch they have created, their daughter plays and grows.

> Brangwen went out to his work, his wife nursed her child and attended in some measure to the farm. They did not think of each other — why should they? Only when she touched him, he knew her instantly, that she was with him, near him . . . When she called, he answered, when he asked, her response came at once, or at length.
>
> Anna's soul was put at peace between them. She looked from one to the other, and she saw them established to her safety, and she was free. She played between [them] in confidence, having the assurance on her right hand and the assurance on her left. She was no longer called upon to uphold with her childish might the broken end of the arch. Her father and her mother now met to the span of the heavens, and she, the child, was free to play in the space between them.
>
> (*The Rainbow*, Penguin edition 1949, p96)

3 The purposes of marriage

Christian teaching over the centuries has summed up the purposes of marriage as (a) to create and nurture children in the finest possible environment — one of love, security and affection; (b) for a man and a woman to offer to each other the sole and permanent right of physical sexual delight;

(c) for the help and support a man and a woman can give to one another when each stands by the other through thick and thin.

According to the Prayer Book

In its marriage service the Church of England Prayer Book of 1928 expresses these three purposes of marriage in this way.

> First, it was ordained for the increase of mankind according to the will of God, and that children might be brought up in the fear and nurture of the Lord, and to the praise of his holy name.
>
> Secondly, it was ordained in order that the natural instincts and affections, implanted by God, should be hallowed and directed aright; that those who are called of God to this holy estate should continue therein in pureness of living.
>
> Thirdly, it was ordained for the mutual society, help, and comfort that the one ought to have of the other, both in prosperity and adversity.

4 Reality

The ideal marriage is not often found within the reality of our daily lives. The number of one-parent families is growing — these are usually single women bringing up their children, and include those women who have chosen not to have abortions when they have found themselves pregnant and unmarried. Some parents choose to stay single.

Single-parent families

As for the permanence of marriage, one in every three British marriages ends in divorce. One in every two American marriages goes the same way. Thirty-five per cent of marriages are in fact remarriages, with one or both partners divorced from their previous spouses. Divorces often result in single-parent families.

Finally, men and women may find themselves bringing up children alone because their marriage partner has died.

5 A Christian defence of desire

Sexual desire can prove immensely powerful, in old and young. In his old age the Greek poet Sophocles was once asked, 'How do you feel about love?' He replied, 'Hush! if you please: to my great delight I have escaped from it, and I feel as if I had escaped from a frantic and savage master.'

Sexual desire helps to cause adultery and persuades men and women to risk sex outside marriage. And because sexual desire is so powerful, the Christian church has often seemed to condemn it outright. This negative attitude was strongly attacked by the Christian poet William Blake, in one of his *Songs of Experience*.

I laid me down upon a bank,
Where love lay sleeping;
I heard among the rushes dank
Weeping, weeping.

Then I went to the heath and the wild,
To the thistles and thorns of the waste;
And they told me how they were beguiled,
Driven out and compelled to be chaste.

I went into the Garden of Love,
And saw what I never had seen!
A Chapel was built in the midst,
Where I used to play on the green.

And the gates of this Chapel were shut,
And 'Thou shalt not' writ over the door;
So I turned to the Garden of Love
That so many sweet flowers bore.

And I saw it was filled with graves,
And tombstones where flowers should be;
And priests in black gowns were walking their rounds,
And binding with briars my joys and desires.

Bearing Blake's poem in mind, none of the arguments used here against indulging in sexuality should be taken to mean that the joys of sex are not, in the eyes of Christians, God-given. The point of controlling something so strong inside us is to let it bring joy rather than pain.

Yet in matters of sex and marriage, so many societies, including our own present-day society, have departed from the ideals of the Bible that three major questions must be faced: how do we regard **sex outside marriage, divorce**, and the **abortion** of unwanted children?

Sex outside marriage

Here is a story from the first book of the Bible about a great Jewish leader named Joseph.

> Now Joseph was well built and handsome, and it happened . . . that his master's wife looked desirously at him and said, 'Sleep with me'. But he refused, and answered his master's wife, 'Because of me, my master does not concern himself with what happens in the house; he has handed over all his possessions to me. He is no more master in this house than I am. He has withheld nothing from me except yourself, because you are his wife. How could I do anything so wicked, and sin against God.' Although she spoke to Joseph day after day he would not agree to sleep with her and surrender to her.
>
> But one day Joseph in the course of his duties came to the house, and there was not a servant there indoors. The woman caught hold of him by his tunic and said, 'Sleep with me'. But he left the tunic in her hand and ran out of the house. Seeing he had left the tunic in her hand and left the house, she called her servants and said to them, 'Look at this! . . . He came to me to sleep with me, but I screamed, and when he heard me scream and shout he left his tunic beside me and ran out of the house. . . .'
>
> When the master heard his wife say, 'This is how your slave treated me', he was furious. Joseph's master had him arrested and committed to the gaol where the king's prisoners were kept. And there in gaol he stayed.
>
> (Genesis chapter 39, verses 7 to 21, JB)

In spite of his misfortune, Joseph is the hero of this story. By not sleeping with his master's wife, he kept two commandments: 'You shall not commit adultery' and 'You shall not covet your neighbour's wife'. In a sense he kept a third of the Ten Commandments: 'You shall not steal,' since committing adultery means stealing another person's spouse.

Adultery condemned

There is no doubt at all that the Jewish Bible, taken up by the Christians, condemns adultery.

1 Adultery

Adultery can deeply hurt the betrayed husband or wife. William Shakespeare put the following words into the mouth of Othello, who supposed that his wife Desdemona had been unfaithful to him.

> O curse of marriage,
> That we call these delicate creatures ours,
> And not their appetites. I had rather be a toad,
> And live upon the vapour of a dungeon,
> Than keep a corner in the thing I love
> For others' uses.

Adultery destroys marriages. In the Christian view it amounts to giving away what no longer belongs to you, your body which you offered to another when you married. 'Let each man have his own wife and each woman her own husband,' counselled St Paul. 'The husband must give his wife what she has the right to expect, and so too the wife to the husband. The wife has no rights over her own body; it is the husband who has them. In the same way, the husband has no rights over his body; the wife has them. (1 Corinthians chapter 7, verses 2 to 4, JB)

None of this is to say that adultery cannot be forgiven. Jesus made this absolutely clear in his words to the woman caught committing adultery (see page 80). But he also made it plain that adultery was a deep wrong. 'Out of the heart come evil intentions: murder, adultery, fornication, theft, perjury, slander,' he declared. 'There are things that make a man unclean.' (Matthew chapter 15, verse 19, JB)

Jesus on adultery

Jesus went further, declaring that even the desire to commit adultery is sinful.

'You have heard how it was said, "You shall not commit adultery",' he said, adding, 'But I say this to you: if a man looks at a woman lustfully, he has already committed adultery with her in his heart.' (Matthew chapter 5, verses 27f, JB)

A crude argument against Jesus's view and *in favour* of sex outside marriage was once put by the philosopher

The lesson of Bertrand Russell

Bertrand Russell, replying to a letter from someone who suggested that this is all right provided that both parties are in love. Russell wrote, 'sex is a need and does not require intense love for its gratification.'

But to gratify sex without regard to any other consideration often hurts, not only others but also yourself. Oddly enough Russell himself had powerfully suffered because of his own sexual promiscuity. In 1915 he had begun to make love to Colette, the wife of the actor Miles Malleson. He took her out and then to his home. 'We talked half the night, and in the middle of the talk we became lovers,' Russell recalled. 'There are those who say one should be prudent, but I do not agree with them. We scarcely knew each other, and yet in that moment there began for both of us a relation profoundly serious and profoundly important, sometimes happy, sometimes painful but never trivial and never unworthy.'

Almost exactly a year later she fell in love with someone else, hoping nevertheless that this would make no difference to her relationship with Bertrand Russell. It did. He was, he wrote, bitterly jealous. 'We had violent quarrels, and things were never again quite the same between us.' For a time, he said, he was tormented with jealousy and driven wild by his sense of impotence. Somehow, he believed, a 'sanctuary' had been 'defiled'. (*The Autobiography of Bertrand Russell*, Vol II, George Allen and Unwin 1968, pp 26 and 37)

Nowhere in his memoirs does Russell suppose that Miles Malleson too might have had such feelings.

2 Sex before marriage

Since the teaching of the Bible reserves physical love-making for marriage, clearly it condemns sex before marriage.

But this is not a sufficient reason for stopping the discussion here and now. Other arguments that have been used for and against enjoying sex before marriage need weighing carefully.

Some do not carry much weight. Obviously enough, those who make love outside marriage risk getting hurt. So do those who marry. If we want a risk-free life, we had better not ever fall in love. And a close relationship between a boy and a girl, a woman and a man, is often an entrancing discovery.

Love is never risk-free

A more powerful argument is that sex before marriage still frequently takes place between those who do not take precautions against conceiving children, and those who feel ready to make love to each other do not by any means always feel ready to commit themselves to marriage and the creation of a new family. This, and the number of divorces in our society, has resulted in far more 'one-parent' families. And of course one-parent families may be caused by the early death of a marriage partner. Those who are left to bring up children alone often need great self-discipline,

One-parent families

A single parent protects and cares for her family.

working extremely hard, cherishing their children, sacrificing much to create a fine home. Even so, the child of a one-parent family may suffer deprivation.

What do we mean here by 'deprivation'? One expert, D W Winnicott, referring to a young girl whose father died before she was born, wrote:

> . . . she had only an idealized father on whom to base her view of man. She had not the experience of being let down gently by a real father.

D W Winnicott continued:

> In her life she easily imagined men to be ideal, which at first had the effect of bringing out the best in them. But sooner or later, inevitably, each man she got to know showed imperfections, and each time this happened she was thrown into a state of despair, and was continually complaining.

Winnicott concludes, 'How much happier she would have been if her father had been alive during her childhood, to be felt by her to be ideal, but also to be found by her to have shortcomings, and to have survived her hate of him when he disappointed her.' (*The Child, the Family and the Outside World*, Penguin Books 1964, p117)

A girl whose life is spoilt to such an extent because she never knew a father is obviously an extreme case. But the lack of either a father or a mother as you are growing up is always significant.

Divorce

The fact that children brought up by only one parent may have problems is an obvious argument against divorce. Yet Protestant churches often understand that divorce can in some situations be the lesser of two evils. Children growing up in a family where the father and mother are continually squabbling or even fighting grow up in an unstable environment.

Other Christian bodies cope with divorce in different ways. Anglicans usually will not remarry divorced people in church, but do admit them as full members of the church. The Eastern Orthodox churches sometimes decree that a marriage has died, even though both partners are still alive. Their reasons include the abandonment of a wife by her husband, adultery by one partner and the impotence of the man. Only the Roman Catholic church remains totally opposed to divorce.

1 Muslims and divorce

What do other great religions teach about divorce? Islamic law by which Muslims live states that a marriage may be brought to an end either by the husband saying so or by the husband and wife together agreeing that it is over. In the second case, the wife usually returns to her husband the dowry he paid when they were married. In addition, if a man marries a second wife, his first wife can declare that he and she are no longer married.

One group of Muslims (those who accept Hanafi law) allow a woman to ask for a dissolution of her marriage:

1 if as a young girl she was married by the agreement of someone other than her father or grandfather;
2 if she was insane when she married;

3 if her husband has gone missing and is over ninety years old;
4 if her husband is impotent.

Also, all Muslims agree that a woman may be legitimately divorced if her husband is suffering from some incurable disease.

2 Jews and divorce

This diversity of opinions about divorce and remarriage is also reflected in the Bible. The Jewish Bible, setting out laws given by Moses, clearly states that a man may divorce his wife if he finds her guilty of some shameful conduct.

> Supposing a man has taken a wife and consummated the marriage; but she has not pleased him and he has found some impropriety of which to accuse her; so he makes out a writ of divorce for her and hands it to her, dismissing her from his house.'
>
> (Deuteronomy chapter 24, verse 1, JB)

Jesus was much stricter. Moses, he said, allowed people to divorce their wives because they were unteachable. 'Now I say this to you,' he continued, 'the man who divorces his wife and marries another is guilty of adultery.' (Matthew chapter 19, verses 8f, JB) Even so, in the same statement, Jesus allowed people to divorce if their husband or wife had been unfaithful to them.

Jesus on divorce

St Paul also wrote that as a last resort divorce was acceptable. He was concerned about Christians married to non-Christians when the non-Christian deserted his or her partner. His own view was that as much as possible Christians married to non-believers should stay with them. 'However,' he added, 'if the unbelieving partner does not agree to this, they may separate. In those circumstances the brother or sister is not tied.' (1 Corinthians chapter 7, verse 15)

Birth control

Today, men and women who are not married and have no intention of marrying are able to enjoy sex without the risk of conceiving children. The various methods of **contraception** also enable happily married couples to decide how many children they want and when they will enjoy bearing and bringing them up.

Roman Catholic view

Many official statements of the Roman Catholic church, however, totally oppose contraception. The reason for this, the church argues, is that those who enjoy sex within marriage must never forget that its primary purpose is to create children. As Pope Pius XI wrote in 1930, the church condemns 'any use whatsoever of matrimony exercised in such a way that the act is deliberately frustrated in its natural power to generate life.' The only way of avoiding conceiving children, the Pope argued, is to abstain from sex altogether. Otherwise we should use our reproductive systems for reproduction.

Protestant view

In the same year the Church of England expressed its disagreement, suggesting that responsible parents ought to limit the size of their families so as to be able to provide them with a secure home, freed from anxieties about money, food and the good things of life. Marriage, the Church of England declared (in line with the view of almost every Protestant church) is more than a means of creating children. It involves quality as well as quantity. The sexual act brings together a man and his wife as no other act can. And Protestants have asked whether there is any meaningful difference between avoiding bearing children by not enjoying intercourse and avoiding it by using contraceptives. Finally, they add, those men married to women far too old to conceive and bear children still love each other sexually. Even the Roman Catholic church does not oppose this sexual love-making, yet it cannot in any way lead to the conception and birth of children.

A further argument offered against the use of contraceptives is that they are 'unnatural', because they are an artificial intrusion into nature's own ways. Opposing this argument, the philosopher Richard Lindlay has written:

> The argument that artificial contraception is wrong simply because it is unnatural is based on the view that, in general, whatever is unnatural is wrong. But this would mean that the use of all sorts of things which benefit mankind and don't harm anybody is wrong. Washing machines and washing powders are made of synthetic materials. They are not 'natural'. If it's wrong to use

Is this your attitude to contraception?

Information on contraception is free to men too. Make the most of the help you can get. 'Phone or visit your doctor or local family planning clinic. Ring the FPA for details.

THE FAMILY PLANNING ASSOCIATION, 27–35 MORTIMER STREET, LONDON W1N 7RJ Tel. 01-636 7866

Designed by Suraj Natarajan, London College of Printing and printed by New Goswell Printing Co Ltd.

Advocating birth-control

things which aren't found naturally, then it's wrong to use washing machines. It would also be immoral to wear synthetic-fibred clothes. But why should anyone think that wearing nylon shirts is immoral?'

(*What Philosophy Does*, Open Books 1978, p3)

Abortion

What, then, happens when a woman learns that she is pregnant but for various reasons decides not to go ahead with the pregnancy. Doctors can terminate the pregnancy with an abortion.

There is considerable evidence that the rate of abortion rises where contraceptives are in scarce supply. For instance, every year one in eight Russian women have abortions. This is twenty-five times greater than the number of abortions in West Germany. In Russia, as opposed to West Germany, there is a chronic shortage of contraceptives.

Legalised abortion

Since 1967 abortion under certain circumstances has been allowed in Britain and is performed in our National Health Service hospitals as well as in many private clinics. The law says that an abortion may be legally performed if, in the opinion of two registered doctors, to continue with the pregnancy would involve more injury to the physical and mental health of the mother than to terminate the pregnancy. In addition, abortions are allowed if there is a substantial risk that if the child were born it would be seriously handicapped by physical or mental abnormalities.

Roman Catholic view

Here again Roman Catholic teaching disagrees with the law. Roman Catholic teaching is that abortion is totally wrong. If an unborn baby is killed indirectly, in an operation to save the life of its mother, that is acceptable. Otherwise, Catholics insist, in no circumstances must you kill an unborn child.

Anglicans take a different line, arguing that if a mother is likely to die in childbirth, it is absurd to look upon the unborn child's life as more valuable than the mother's. The mother has responsibilities and value as a wife. She may already have children to care for. To regard her life as less valuable than that of the unborn child (says a Church of England report of 1965) 'does not consider the mother's "right to live" in terms of her wider roles of wife or mother (actual or potential) of other children, as well as in terms of her own person.' (*Abortion, an Ethical Discussion*, Church Information Office 1965, p33)

A further argument in favour of legal abortion is that it stops illegal ones, which are extremely risky for the women who undergo them, since those who perform these abortions are in no way controlled by the law.

Back-street abortion

Before the 1967 Act legalised some abortions in Britain, 'back-street abortions', as they are called, frequently resulted in the death of the mother. As a Roman Catholic politician wrote in 1963, 'If it could be established that a change in the law would get rid of dangerous abortions there would be a case for its alteration. The state would not be approving abortion but merely removing a penal sanction in the interests of public health.' (Norman St John-Stevas *The Right to Life*, 1963, p41) The following year 5,958 women were admitted to London hospitals as emergency cases after illegal abortions. The year the Abortion Act of 1967 came into force, only five British women died as the result of illegal abortions.

Is abortion murder?

In Britain legally it isn't. Yet we must still ask what is being killed when an unborn child is aborted. Normally we regard it as civilised to protect the weak. This is specifically laid down as a Christian principle in the New Testament. Obviously, an unborn child (or foetus) is totally unable to care for itself, 'weak' in every sense.

What we have to decide is whether, in aborting this foetus, we are killing a fellow human being. Fully grown babies who have not yet emerged from their mothers' wombs are clearly human beings. To kill them is undoubtedly to kill a member of the human race.

But is the union of a male sperm and a female ovum also a person, from the moment it is conceived? Is a microscopic cell or a fertilised egg, inside a pregnant woman, a person? If not, when does this fertilised egg become a person?

When does the fertilised egg become a person.

Some people say it becomes a person almost immediately it is conceived. Helmut Thielicke, the Lutheran theologian, supported that argument. Since the foetus has its own circulatory system and its own brain, 'These elementary biological facts should be sufficient to establish its status as a human being,' he wrote. (*The Ethics of Sex*, 1964, p228) Others disagree. For instance, the American Joseph Fletcher flatly asserted in 1955 that 'an embryo in therapeutic abortion has no personal value or development at stake.' (*Morals and Medicine*, 1955, p205)

It is hard to see what scientific basis there is for these apparently confident, if contradictory statements. Yet when it comes to deciding for or against and abortion, it is vital for us to work out which side we will support. Either the doctors who perform the abortion are simply removing an unthinking, unfeeling bundle of protoplasm from the mother's womb, or they are killing a human being capable of experiencing sensations.

Euthanasia

Questions about the deliberate killing of an unborn foetus are parallelled by the problems raised when a member of a family (usually an old person) is dying of a painful or undignified and incurable illness. Should people in this state be allowed to ask their doctors to hasten their death?

This much-disputed form of killing is known as 'euthanasia'. The word itself means an 'easy death', and euthanasia almost aways refers to gently ending the life either of the aged or of those who are terminally ill with some painful disease.

George V

Some of the most exalted persons in Britain have been painlessly killed by their doctors. For instance, Lord Dawson, physician of Sandringham to the British king, George V, gave the king a fatal dose of drugs at the end of his life. George V was seriously and painfully ill. There was no chance of his recovery. Lord Dawson wrote, 'Hours of waiting just for the mechanical end when all that is really life has departed only exhausts the onlookers and keeps them so strained that they cannot avail themselves of the solace of thought, communion or prayer.'

Lord Dawson was not thinking solely of the peace of mind of the king's relatives. He wrote of his patient's right of 'dignity and serenity' at the end of his life, all demanding 'a brief final scene'. So he killed the king, by injecting three-quarters of a gram of morphia into his jugular vein. This was, as Dawson put it, 'so-called euthanasia on which almost silently agreement now exists.'

Is there silent agreement? Lord Dawson did not consult the opinion of the man he killed; George V was too far advanced on the road to death to be consulted. In his case euthanasia was certainly not voluntary.

1 Voluntary euthanasia

In Britain the Voluntary Euthanasia Society was formed in 1935 to campaign for a man's or a woman's right to seek an 'easy death'. Since the greatest objection to euthanasia is that it might not be voluntary, the society strives to bring about a situation in which any responsible adult suffering from a fatal and distressing illness can receive an immediate and painless death only at his or her considered request.

Today many members of the Voluntary Euthanasia Society always carry with them cards stating that in the event of a medical emergency they do not wish to be resuscitated or have their lives artificially prolonged if this would lead to their lingering for days or even months in pain or mental anguish. Holland is the country where such practices are most widespread. It has been estimated that 8 per cent of of the total number of deaths are the result of doctors killing terminally or terribly ill patients at their own request.

In Holland

In 1985 a poll showed that 72 per cent of the British population agrees with this aim. Even a majority of members of the main religious bodies agree. The Methodist leader Dr Leslie Weatherhead once wrote:

> I sincerely believe that those who come after us will wonder why on earth we kept a human being alive against his will, when all the dignity, beauty and meaning of life had vanished; when any gain to anyone was clearly impossible and when we should have been punished by the State if we kept an animal alive in similar physical conditions.

2 Problems about euthanasia

The Voluntary Euthanasia Society itself raises questions about its own policy — all of which must be considered before anyone decides for or against euthanasia. These questions include:

- Would the legalisation of euthanasia put too much power into the hands of doctors?
- If voluntary euthanasia were legalised, how could we be sure it would not lead to moral pressure being applied to sick people who were a burden to their relatives?
- Might not the legalisation of voluntary euthanasia lead to involuntary euthanasia of the old or handicapped?
- Is it not our duty to look after sick people and make them happy so that they will not want to cut their lives short?
- Isn't life still precious, no matter what sort of life it is?
- Can we really tell when a patient's condition is hopeless? Are not cures being invented all the time?
- Suppose you asked for voluntary euthanasia and then changed your mind: would it be too late?
- Could voluntary euthanasia help in cases of senile dementia — a prospect that to many people is the worst fear of all?

3 The Bible

'If we live, we live for the Lord; and if we die, we die for the Lord,' wrote St Paul, 'so that alive or dead we belong to the Lord.' (Romans chapter 14, verse 8, JB). Christians have frequently taken such statements to mean that it is God who gives us life and he alone should have the right to take it away.

Modern medicines predicament

On this view euthanasia, whether voluntary or not, is always wrong. At the same time Christians have accepted the fact that modern medical techniques can absurdly prolong an earthly life that otherwise would undoubtedly be over. Victims of road accidents, for example, are frequently put on life-support machines when they reach hospital. In theory in this way they could be kept 'alive' indefinitely. If however the doctors then discover that the victim's brain is dead, no conceivable good is gained from keeping the heart and lungs going. The victim can never recover. In such a case, no one would quarrel with the doctors switching off the life-support machine.

4 Care of the elderly

The question of euthanasia raises in an acute form our

responsibility for the elderly in our society. Take widows, for instance. The Old and New Testaments leave no doubt that first their own families and secondly society in general has a duty to care for them.

Care of widows

'Be considerate to widows,' teaches St Paul. 'If a widow has children or grandchildren, they are to learn first of all to do their duty to their own families and repay their debt to their parents, because this is what pleases God . . . Anyone who does not look after his own relations, especially if they are living with him, has rejected the faith and is worse than an unbeliever.' (1 Timothy chapter 5, verses 3f and 8, JB)

At the very start of the Christian church, some Christians in Jerusalem pointed out that a number of their widows were being overlooked during the daily distribution of food. The church leaders appointed seven men of good reputation especially to remedy this and see that no widow went short. (Acts of the Apostles chapter 6, verses 1 to 6, JB)

Respect for one's own family

Here the first Christians were putting into practice and extending the ancient laws of the Jews, set out in God's commandment, 'Honour your father and your mother', and repeated many times later in the Bible. To honour someone is to take them seriously, to recognise their importance and not to underestimate them. 'Listen to your father who begot you, despise not your mother in her old age,' says a Jewish proverb. 'May you be the joy of your father, the gladness of her who bore you!' (Proverbs chapter 23, verses 22 and 25)

The wisdom of age

In today's world the old still bear rich wisdom and experience, even though the world has changed so rapidly in the past half-century that they themselves often feel out-of-date and sometimes unsure of themselves. The young should still be able to respect age, and above all the older members of their own family.

Parents and children, husbands and wives

'Wives, give way to your husbands, as you should in the Lord. Husbands, love your wives and treat them with gentleness. Children, be obedient to your parents always, because that is what will please the Lord. Parents, never

Young and old caring for each other in a close family

drive your children to resentment or you will make them feel frustrated.' (Colossians chapter 3, verses 18 to 21, JB). Although few today would suggest that wives should always give way to their husbands, St Paul's words still illustrate the mutual respect necessary in a family that gives each member his or her full due.

They do not mean that children should not be given freedom to grow up and finally to leave the intimate family circle. When we discussed marriage, we discovered the Bible speaking about leaving one's father and mother to set up a new family.

Jesus

The example of Jesus himself reveals that those who do not marry (as he never did) still need to make their own way in the world like other children, and must be allowed to do so by their parents. When he was 12 years old he and his family went to Jerusalem. He stayed behind in the Temple, even though Mary and Joseph were looking for him everywhere. (They thought at first that he was with their relatives and friends somewhere in the whole group.)

After three days of searching, they discovered Jesus in the Temple, listening to the Jewish teachers there and asking them questions. Mary asked Jesus, 'My child, why have you done this to us? See how worried your father and I have been, looking for you.' He replied, 'Why were you looking for me? Did you not know that I must be busy with my Father's affairs?' (Luke chapter 2, verses 41 to 50, JB)

St Luke, who tells us this story, says that Jesus's parents did not understand what he meant. Yet Jesus returned with them to their home at Nazareth, continuing to live under their authority. Growing up, increasing in wisdom, learning new ways which are not the ways of one's parents, need not mean a rift or split in the home. But while this is happening there will inevitably be some tensions in the family.

By the time Jesus came to be killed, Mary's husband Joseph may well have died, since we hear nothing about him in the accounts of the crucifixion.

Jesus cares for his mother

What we do read about is the way that Jesus, even as he was hanging on the cross, did everything possible to care for his mother, entrusting her to one of his best-loved followers. 'Near the cross of Jesus stood his mother and his mother's sister, Mary the wife of Clopas, and Mary of Magdala,' St John tells us. 'Seeing his mother and the disciple he loved standing near her, Jesus said to his mother, "Woman, this is your son". Then to the disciple he said, "This is your mother". And from that moment the disciple made a place for her in his home.' (John chapter 19, verses 25 to 27, RSV)

Visions of a good society

This ideal of a family at peace, each caring for the other, can be extended to the whole of society. The Bible is full of visions of how God's people can live together. Here are three.

Kings of the earth and all people:
princes and all judges of the world;
Young men and maidens, old men and children,
praise the name of the Lord.

(Psalm 148, verses 11f, JB)

The virgin will take pleasure in the dance,
young men and old will be happy.

(Jeremiah chapter 31, verse 31, JB)

Old men and old women will again sit down
in the squares of Jerusalem;
every one of them staff in hand
because of their great age.
And the squares of the city will be full
of boys and girls
playing in the squares.

(Zechariah chapter 8, verses 4f, JB)

As these visions teach, a society can live in harmony only when all its members, young and old, men and women, are properly respected. And each makes his own different contribution to the rest. In such a society even the weakest, the children playing in the squares, add to happiness.

Threats to social life

In Britain well over 90 per cent of the adult population drink alcohol, either occasionally or frequently. The law forbids persons under 18 to drink in a pub or bar, or to buy alcohol. To be drunk in a public place is an offence, as is to drive while even moderately drunk.

Medical risks of alcohol

Medically it is considered safe to drink the equivalent of four pints of beer a day if you are a man and three pints if you are a woman. Fewer than five per cent of the adult population exceed this. Those who do risk damaging their livers and their brains, as well as bringing on heart diseases and ulcers. The worst situation is that of alcoholics, those men and women psychologically dependent on drink and suffering anxiety, trembling and even delirium if they cannot get it.

1 The use and abuse of alcohol

Wine, as the Bible says, is able to make men's hearts glad (Psalm 104, verse 15).

But since it can also be abused, the same Bible warns against it (as against all forms of greed).

Do not be one of those forever tippling wine
nor one of those who gorge themselves with meat;
for a drunkard and a glutton impoverish themselves,
and a drowsy head makes a wearer of rags . . .

Never relish how red it is, this wine,
how sparkling it is in the cup,
how smooth its flow.
In the end its bite is like a serpent's,
its sting as sharp as an adder's.
Your eyes will see strange things,
distorted words will come from your heart.
You will be like one sleeping in mid ocean,
like one asleep at the mast-head.'
(Proverbs chapter 23, verses 20f and 31 to 34, JB)

2 Drug abuse

Risks of tobacco-smoking

Alcohol and cigarettes are the most common drugs in Western society. Just as those who drink too much risk damaging their God-given bodies, so tobacco-smoking is responsible for at least 100,000 premature deaths in Britain every year. Lung cancer and infections, blood clots, strokes and heart attacks are all made more likely by smoking.

And as with alcohol, it is alarmingly possible to become dependent on cigarettes, unable to do without one for long. Each time a dependent smoker puts one cigarette into his or her mouth, statistically that person's life is shortened by five and a half minutes.

Seeing their elders smoking and drinking, many young people have felt no qualms at indulging in other drugs, all of which are more or less harmful. Unlike alcohol and tobacco, all these other drugs are illegal in Britain.

'speed'

Amphetamines (known as 'speed') can be sniffed or injected. Their effect is at first pleasant. Users are more alert, livelier, slightly giggly. Soon afterwards many become depressed, unable to sleep, feeling at the same time persecuted. **Cannabis** (called 'dope' or 'pot') is smoked and produces intoxication, hilarity, talkativeness and often a heightened sense of sound and colours. No one knows the long-term effects of cannabis, but **Cocaine** ('coke'), a white powder which is usually sniffed, produces first relaxation and pleasure, then far less acceptable irrational fears and extreme anxiety. Cocaine is also likely to become essential for the user's supposed wellbeing, at the same time as it is harming his or her body.

'dope'

'coke'

'acid'

LSD (or 'acid') is a white powder taken as a tablet or even on sugar cubes. After an hour and a half or so the user begins his or her LSD trip, which can last up to 12 hours.

The danger of drugs

LSD trips produce widely contrary experiences in the user. For some people a trip can be exhilarating, even ecstatic. For others it produces panic and utter disorientation. **Heroin** (also known as 'skag' or 'smack') is a powder heated to give off fumes, which are then inhaled. At first the user feels far more alert, but this is soon followed by drowsiness. Such effects relieve users of stress, but frequent use leads to dependence and an overdose can kill. Finally, several sorts of **mushrooms** send users on trips in which hilarity and excitement often combine with extraordinary dreams and images. High doses of these 'magic mushrooms' can produce what are known as 'bad trips', in which the user suffers vomiting and nausea instead of the expected pleasures.

'smack'

'magic mushrooms'.

Work and leisure

Work can be fun; it can also be drudgery. The Bible sees it as both; but its main emphasis is to urge us to work happily: 'Whatever your work is, put your heart into it as if it were for the Lord and not for men,' wrote St Paul (Colossians chapter 3, verse 23, JB). He would warn his followers to keep out of the company of those who were lazy.

St Paul on work

To work hard enables a man or woman to help those who cannot earn enough themselves. Again St Paul puts it clearly. 'We must exert ourselves to support the weak, remembering the words of the Lord Jesus, who himself said, "There is more happiness in giving than in receiving".' (Acts of the Apostles chapter 20, verse 35, JB)

Everyone in Paul's view had a different contribution to make to the good of society. We all need each other, just as different parts of the human body — weak and strong — combine to make a perfect human being. Eyes need hands and heads need feet. In fact, as St Paul once said, 'it is precisely those parts of the body that seem to be the weakest which are the indispensable ones' (1 Corinthians chapter 12, verse 22, JB). So the people in society who *seem* to be the weakest may well be the most valuable.

Unemployment

St Paul also went so far as to say that anyone who wouldn't

work shouldn't eat (2 Thessalonians chapter 3, verse 10). But in many of our great cities today a new problem has arisen: quite simply many cannot find work.

Enforced leisure

Being out of work can badly affect other aspects of our social lives. Drug-taking (save for smoking tobacco) is emphatically a leisure-time existence. On the whole we don't (or can't) drink or use cannabis and manage to work well. Drug-taking and increased drinking are undoubtedly encouraged by the fact that many of us today suffer enforced leisure because we can find no work.

Effects

The effect of being unemployed — quite apart from problems it creates about money — can be extremely disturbing. People begin to think they count for nothing. Whereas they once would try to change jobs to find a more satisfying way of life, they begin to feel they would take any job, however unsatisfying, to get back into work.

All of us need to feel an accepted part of the society in which we live. We need the 'esteem' of society (though those who feel they need to be envied as well do not have a well-developed social sense).

Jobs can offer various satisfactions: a sense of security; a sense of worth; money; esteem in the community; workmates; the opportunity to make one's own contribution to our society; the deep pleasure of achieving something worthwhile; even a share in the way important decisions are made for tomorrow's world. Jobs help to keep the older members of our society fit and alert. Taking a job helps a young person to feel that he or she is becoming an adult.

Is it right that today's society often denies even the least of these satisfactions to some of its members?

Other answers

As the Anglican Bishop of Liverpool, David Sheppard, has written, unemployment seems to take away a man or woman's opportunity to make a useful contribution to society and receive recognition from that society. But he adds, 'Perhaps paid work is not the only way. Thinking of those who have least opportunity for being recognized, it will not do to say, "We'll pay you to stay alive. But we don't really need you or your skills at all."' (*Bias to the Poor*, Hodder and Stoughton 1983, p112) At the same time, the bishop noted, full employment seems unlikely to be a normal feature of our society again for many years to come — if ever.

New questions

Among the many questions that this raises are:

- What sort of social wage should be paid to those who cannot find decent work?

- Is there new scope for helping the workless to serve the community by improving the environment — clearing canals, creating gardens and the like?
- What kinds of leisure activities can we encourage, not just as what we do in our our 'time off' but as essential for human wellbeing?
- How can a man or woman feel creative and useful without having a regular job?
- Why can't we share such jobs as we do have?
- How can we teach that we are all of value, in fact of *equal* value in the sight of God, whether we're able to work or not?

Recreation

Lastly, can we ever begin to see recreation as more important than work?

In a letter of 1895, George Bernard Shaw wrote to his friend Janet Achurch that 'recreation is the secret of the religious life — of the old cathedral building. You go in there and pray or meditate, and you are profoundly rested and recreated. You do this every day . . . you live the heavenly life, and die at a stupendous age, unexhausted in spirit.'

Useful addresses

Alcoholics Anonymous, General Services Office, PO Box 1, Stonebow House, Stonebow, York YO1 2NJ (tel 0904 644026)

Families Anonymous, 88 Caledonian Road, London N7 9DN (tel 01–278 8805)

Help the Aged, St James's Walk, London EC1R 0EE (tel 01–253 0253)

National Marriage Guidance Council, Herbert College, Little Church Street, Rugby, Warwickshire CV21 3AP (tel 0788 73241)

SCODA (Standing Conference on Drug Abuse), 1–4 Hatton Place, London EC1N 8ND (tel dial 100 and ask for Freefone 'Drug Problems')

The Voluntary Euthanasia Society, 18 Prince of Wales Terrace, London W8 5PG (tel 01–937 7770)

Questions and coursework

1 Jesus said 'What God has joined together, man must not ....

2 In the Bible children are told 'Honour your .... and ....

3 In Britain one in every three marriages end in ....

4 One commandment given to us in the Bible is 'You shall not commit ....'

5 Men and women who make love but do not wish to conceive children can prevent this by various methods of birth control which involve using ....

6 Destroying a foetus while it is in its mother's womb is known as ....

7 Euthanasia means an ....

8 What are the two most common drugs used in Western society?

9 Name three drugs that are banned by law in Britain.

10 St Paul observed, 'There is more happiness in .... than in receiving.'

11 What do we learn about divorce in the Sermon on the Mount? Do we as a society today accept this teaching?

12 What is the meaning of adultery? Give some reasons why adultery is forbidden.

13 'I could not continue to live with you if you were unfaithful to me.' Discuss this attitude with reference to *two* different points of view about it, one of which must be religious.

14 'It is the children I feel sorry for when parents separate.' Do you agree with this statement? Give reasons for and against the view that couples should stay together for the sake of the children.

15 'People give up too easily; widespread adultery and easy divorce are signs of a rotten society.' Discuss whether stricter laws or a refusal of all churches/religions to remarry divorced people would be an advantage.

16 Not all Christians agree about divorce and remarriage. State *two* opposing views and say which one you agree with.

17 Give two different religious views about birth control.

18 Describe a wedding ceremony and explain how the promises made during the ceremony should affect the rest of the married couple's life.

19 Describe three methods of birth control.
20 'Do not commit adultery.' Name two problems which are caused in today's society when this commandment is broken.
21 Since 1967 abortion under certain circumstances has been allowed in Britain. What are these circumstances? Give the reasons why the Roman Catholic church disagrees.
22 What is 'euthanasia'? What is 'voluntary euthanasia'? Define the problems involved with both.
23 'It is God who gives us life and he alone should have the right to take it away.' Comment on this statement.
24 'How can we teach that we are all of value — in fact of *equal* value — in the sight of God, whether we are able to work or not?' How would you deal with this question?
25 A meeting has been called in your area to discuss a plan to convert a local house into a centre for the rehabilitation of drug addicts. This plan has aroused much publicity and many of the residents in the neighbourhood are objecting to it.
   (a) Explain what is meant by the phrase 'the rehabilitation of drug addicts'.
   (b) Name two organisations that are concerned with helping drug addicts.
   (c) Outline two objections which might be made against the plan, and assess these objections in the light of Christian principles.
   (d) Suggest two points that might be made by a speaker in favour of the plan and assess these in the light of Christian principles.
26 Do a survey of the town in which you live, to discover the work done by the churches to help the aged.
27 'Honour your father and your mother.' What is your full understanding of this commandment?
28 How would a Christian describe the differences between sex and love?
29 Give three reasons why marriages break down.
30 Divorce can bring many problems to a family. State three of them. How would you advise someone whose marriage is breaking down?

6 Choosing Right from Wrong

Why be moral?

On the way out of a large department store you pay your bill for some new, fairly expensive clothes. Later you discover that you were given far too much change. Your reaction is: (1) to keep the money without giving it a second thought; (2) to keep the money, reasoning that the shop makes a large enough profit anyway, and that the cashiers at the check-out probably give many people too little change as well as sometimes making the mistake of giving too much; (3) to go and give the money back?

Keeping the change

Here is another situation. You work part-time on a market-stall, selling vegetables. The boss tells you that he can't make enough profit to pay you unless the scales are not quite right. When someone buys, say, a kilo of bananas, they actually get under a kilo. What is your response: (1) accept the boss's instruction, since you don't want to lose your job; (2) try to change the boss's mind, arguing that dishonesty simply isn't right, but adding that you don't want to lose your job and if he insists, you'll do what he says; (3) resign and tell the local weights and measures office why?

Tipping the scales

These two situation raise the whole basic question of the way we have to deal with all the issues discussed in this book. They simply ask, why be moral?

In both situations clearly most people would reply that option 3 is the moral thing to do. Option 1 is the easiest choice, since it offers a quiet life, and a profitable one. And option 2, in both cases, takes a line midway between absolute morality and utter selfishness. Option 3 is saying, let's be honest whatever it costs.

1 Doing what we feel like

What makes us say that option 1 is the moral one? Some philosophers have argued that we simply don't know. 'If I am asked, "What is good?", wrote G E Moore, 'my answer is that good is good, and that is the end of the matter. Or if I am asked, "How is good to be defined?" my answer is that it cannot be defined, and that is all I have to say about it.'

Other distinguished philosophers have argued that our ideas of right and wrong are simply how we feel. Professor Alfred Ayer wrote: 'Since ethical judgments are mere expressions of feeling, there can be no way of determining the validity of an ethical system, and indeed, no sense in asking whether any such system is true.'

But if morality cannot be argued about, how do you prove that, for instance, letting millions die of hunger is wrong? G E Moore would have said that we simply know that it is wrong to let them die, though we can't prove it. But what do you say to someone who equally simply argues, 'It's nothing to do with me. I don't care'?

If morality is just a matter of feeling, how for instance do you argue with someone who says of casual sex, 'I don't mind what it does to other people; I take it when I feel like it'? Don't we have to take into account other people's feelings as well as our own?

Appealing to Christian teaching

Christian teaching leaves no doubt that we must. St Paul puts it clearly: Christians are free men and women, but they must not misuse their freedom. 'Be careful, or this liberty will lead to self-indulgence. Serve one another, rather, in works of love, since the whole of the Law is summarised in a single command: "Love your neighbour as yourself". If you go snapping at each other and tearing each other to pieces, you had better watch or you will destroy the whole community.' (Galatians chapter 5, verses 13 to 15, JB)

The two great commandments

'Love your neighbour as yourself' is an Old Testament rule (from Leviticus chapter 9, verse 18), which had already been singled out by Jesus himself as the essence of God's law. To complete it, Jesus added another Old Testament law (from Deuteronomy chapter 6, verses 4f, JB):

> Listen, Israel, the Lord our God is one Lord, and you must love the Lord your God with all your heart, and with all your soul and with all your mind and with all your strength.

Jesus said, 'There is no commandment greater than these.' (Mark chapter 12, verses 29 to 31, JB)

2 The Ten Commandments

The Jews and Christians both regarded as specially important ten commandments given to them by God through their great leader Moses. These run:

> I am the Lord your God who brought you out of the land of Egypt, out of the house of bondage. You shall have no other Gods before me.
>
> You shall not make for yourself any graven image, or any likeness of anything that is in heaven above, or that is in the earth beneath, or that is in the water under the earth. You shall not bow down to them nor serve them . . .
>
> You shall not take the name of the Lord your God in vain.
>
> Remember the seventh day to keep it holy. On six days you shall labour and do all your work; but the seventh day is the sabbath of the Lord your God. In it you shall not do any work, neither you, nor your son, nor your daughter, nor your manservant, nor your maidservant, nor your cattle, nor the stranger who is within your gates . . .
>
> Honour your father and your mother, so that your days may be long upon the land which the Lord your God gives you.
>
> You shall not murder.
>
> You shall not commit adultery.
>
> You shall not steal.
>
> You shall not bear false witness against your neighbour.
>
> You shall not covet your neighbour's house, you shall not covet your neighbour's wife, nor his manservant, nor his maidservant, nor his ox, nor his ass, nor anything that is your neighbour's.
>
> (Exodus chapter 20, verses 1 to 17, RSV)

These 'Ten Commandments' have formed the basis of much of the moral teaching of the Jewish and Christian worlds.

3 Why 'ought' we to do something? Why 'must' we?

The question remains, why? Why shouldn't we covet out neighbour's wife? Why shouldn't we steal? Why shouldn't we murder or lie about our neighbour?

One problem about proving why we should behave

morally arises over the way we talk. We say, 'You *ought* to tell the truth.' We say, 'You *must* love your neighbour.' We say, 'You *should* care for the poor and needy.' To do so, we say, is *right* and *good*. Not to do so is *wrong* and *bad*.

But where do these ideas of 'right', 'wrong', 'good', 'bad', 'must', 'should' and the rest come from?

David Hume

If you look at any action, all you can see is what is happening. You can't actually see 'good' or 'bad' in it. A Scottish philosopher called David Hume put it like this: if you consider what everyone thinks wrong, say, vicious murder, you cannot see in the murder itself anything called 'vice'.

Instead, the philosopher wrote, 'you find only certain passions, motives, volitions and thoughts. The vice entirely escapes you, as long as you consider the object.'

The moral judgment we make about murder, said Hume, comes from within ourselves. Looking for 'vice' in the action of murder itself is useless. 'You can never find it, till you turn your reflexion into your own breast, and find a sentiment of disapprobation, which arises in you, towards this action.' Our ideas of morality come from inside us, from the way we look at things.

Morality and human nature

Our minds, some thinkers believe, are already filled with ideas not learned from experience. These ideas include the notion of right and wrong. Although people might disagree about what is right and what is wrong, no one disagrees that you should try to follow what is right and avoid wrongdoing.

King Darius's story

A famous story about King Darius of Persia illustrates this. Darius knew of Indians who made a meal of their dead parents. He also knew that the Greeks found this idea abominable. He therefore asked a group of Greeks how much money he would have to pay them before they would eat their dead fathers. They answered that no amount of money could persuade them to do this. Then he asked the Indians how much money they would need to bribe them to cremate their dead fathers. They became extremely angry, telling Darius not even to speak of such a thing.

The point of the story is that despite the quite different behaviour of the Greeks and the Indians, both possessed deeply engraved feelings of what is right and what is wrong.

Although people may disagree about what they should do and how they should behave, nobody really believes it doesn't matter.

Kant's law

Taking this idea further, the German philosopher Immanuel Kant insisted that we all possess in our minds pure principles for understanding the world. For instance, we all believe that whatever happens, something else caused it, even though no one can ever prove this about *everything*.

Kant's basic moral principle

Kant also said that these principles for understanding the world include moral principles. He set out what in his view was the chief one, basically that anything you wish to do is moral only if you would not mind if everybody else acted in the same way.

Kant's law helps us to answer, for example, the question we have just asked: how to deal with someone who says of casual sex, 'I don't mind what it does to other people; I take it when I feel like it'? Suppose that became a universal principle, with everyone behaving in this way. Far more people would get hurt than not. The speaker would be as likely to suffer as anyone else.

The same goes for personal violence. Before I decide it is all right for me to beat up anyone I like, I have to ask what would happen if everybody came to the same decision.

Happiness

Little happiness would come from everyone following his or her own self-interest. On the other hand, there is no reason why behaving morally should mean that you can't be happy.

Over the centuries, men and women have offered systems of morality promising to promote human happiness. Jesus himself set out one of his most remarkable descriptions of true Christianity by suggesting that only those behaving in this way would find true happiness. He said:

> How happy are the poor in spirit;
> theirs is the kingdom of heaven.
> Happy are the gentle;
> they shall have the earth for their heritage.

Blessed are the merciful. Surgeon Pauline Cutting treated the wounded in a refugee camp in Beirut despite facing starvation and shellfire.

Happy are those who mourn;
they shall be comforted.
Happy are those who hunger and thirst for what is right;
they shall be satisfied.
Happy are the merciful;
they shall have mercy shown them.
Happy are the pure in heart;
they shall see God.
Happy are the peacemakers;
they shall be called the sons of God.
Happy are those who are persecuted in the cause of right;
theirs is the kingdom of heaven.
Happy are you when people abuse you and persecute you and speak all kinds of calumny against you on my account. Rejoice and be glad, for your reward will be great in heaven.

(Matthew chapter 5, verses 2 to 12, JB)

So Jesus suggests, seeking what is right leads in the end to happiness.

1 Hedonism

Moral behaviour based on what makes you happiest is often called 'hedonism'. Hedonism is not, however, what Jesus is teaching here. Hedonists hold that pleasure is the only thing that is good. Pain, they add, is the only evil.

Pain is the only evil

Obviously Jesus is not saying this, since he believes true happiness might involve willingly suffering for what it right. Hedonists would reject this.

Hedonism is far closer to egoism, the notion that individual self-interest is all that matters. An egoist straightforwardly says, 'All that counts is what helps me. Therefore everyone else should behave in a way that looks after my interests.'

2 Egoism

As it stands, this obviously doesn't make sense as a moral code, since only one person in the world could be the complete egoist, with the rest of the world's population his or her slaves.

But some people have argued that, if you rewrite egoism to mean 'Everyone should act in his or her own interests', then the rule works. It is not in anyone's interest to behave so viciously that no one else will put up with them. It is not in my interest to drive on any side of the road I choose, since inevitably some other driver will smash into me.

If we all act in ways that truly further our own interest, that means taking other people's interest into account. So then, it is claimed, everyone will be better off.

This, alas, is not true. Egoism in fact cannot work if everyone selfishly follows his or her own inclinations. If a notice in the park reads, 'Please do not walk on the grass,' I may argue: 'It doesn't ruin the park lawns if only I walk on the grass.' So I secretly do so. Then I find that everyone else makes the same calculation, with the result that the grass becomes mud.

A more difficult example

If only two people each behave in their own interest, even that is sometimes enough to make life worse for both of them.

Suppose, for example, the police capture two terrorists. The police desperately want to find out more about the terrorists' connections. The terrorists are kept apart from each other. As a bribe, the police tell each terrorist that if one of them tells everything he will be released. If he refuses to betray his accomplices, he will be jailed for life. On the other hand, if both terrorists decide to split on the organisation they work for, the police will release neither, but keep them jailed for only 10 years. Now, each terrorist will clearly calculate that the best thing to do is tell all, regardless of what his fellow terrorist does. But because both follow their own individual interests, both end up worse than if only one of them were an egoist.

In short, egoism as a moral philosophy simply doesn't make sense.

Morality and pleasure

Yet some thinkers have produced theories of morality which, although based on the search for pleasure and the avoidance of pain, are far from mere selfish hedonism or egoism. The two most important and famous of these theories are those put forward by an ancient Greek, Epicurus, and an Englishman named Jeremy Bentham.

1 Epicureanism

The teachings of Epicurus are known as Epicureanism. Egoism and Epicureanism are often confused. Epicureanism is far less selfish and much more attractive.

It is named after the ancient Greek who taught it: Epicurus was born in 341 BC and died 72 years later. He had a remarkable gift for friendship and at the age of 32 he set up in the city of Athens a school, in his own garden, to which he welcomed his friends and followers. Unlike most teachers in ancient Greece, Epicurus brought into his school not only women but also a favourite slave whom everybody called Mouse. (When Epicurus died, it was found that in his will he had freed all his slaves.)

The school was admired throughout the known world, and for several centuries many men and women who lived good lives copied Epicurus's ways and taught his philosophy.

Certainly Epicurus believed that (as he wrote) 'pleasure is the be-all and end-all of life.' But his idea of pleasure was not the selfishness of the egoist. Epicurus taught that some pleasures are not worth having, for in the end they produce pain. Pleasures which anger or harm your fellow men and women ultimately rebound on you, and the misery that results far outweighs the original joy.

Some pleasures produce pain

To avoid pain was, in the view of Epicurus, essential for anyone who sought pleasure. So he believed in moderation, not excess. Instead of total self-indulgence in drink, for instance, everyone in his school drank water apart from half a pint of wine a day. The greatest pleasure anyone could achieve, Epicurus taught, came from not asking for more than was possible. Above all, it consisted in leading a peaceful life amidst ones friends.

For Epicurus, then, pleasure really means a healthy body and an untroubled spirit. The idea that he taught utter selfishness is totally wrong. Debauchery, greed, massive self-indulgence all harm the body. Striving for more than you need in life will never lead to a tranquil mind. Friendship offers the greatest joy we can attain, and (Epicurus taught) there may even be times when men or women should sacrifice their own interests for the sake of their friends.

2 Jeremy Bentham

The Englishman who systematically made happiness the

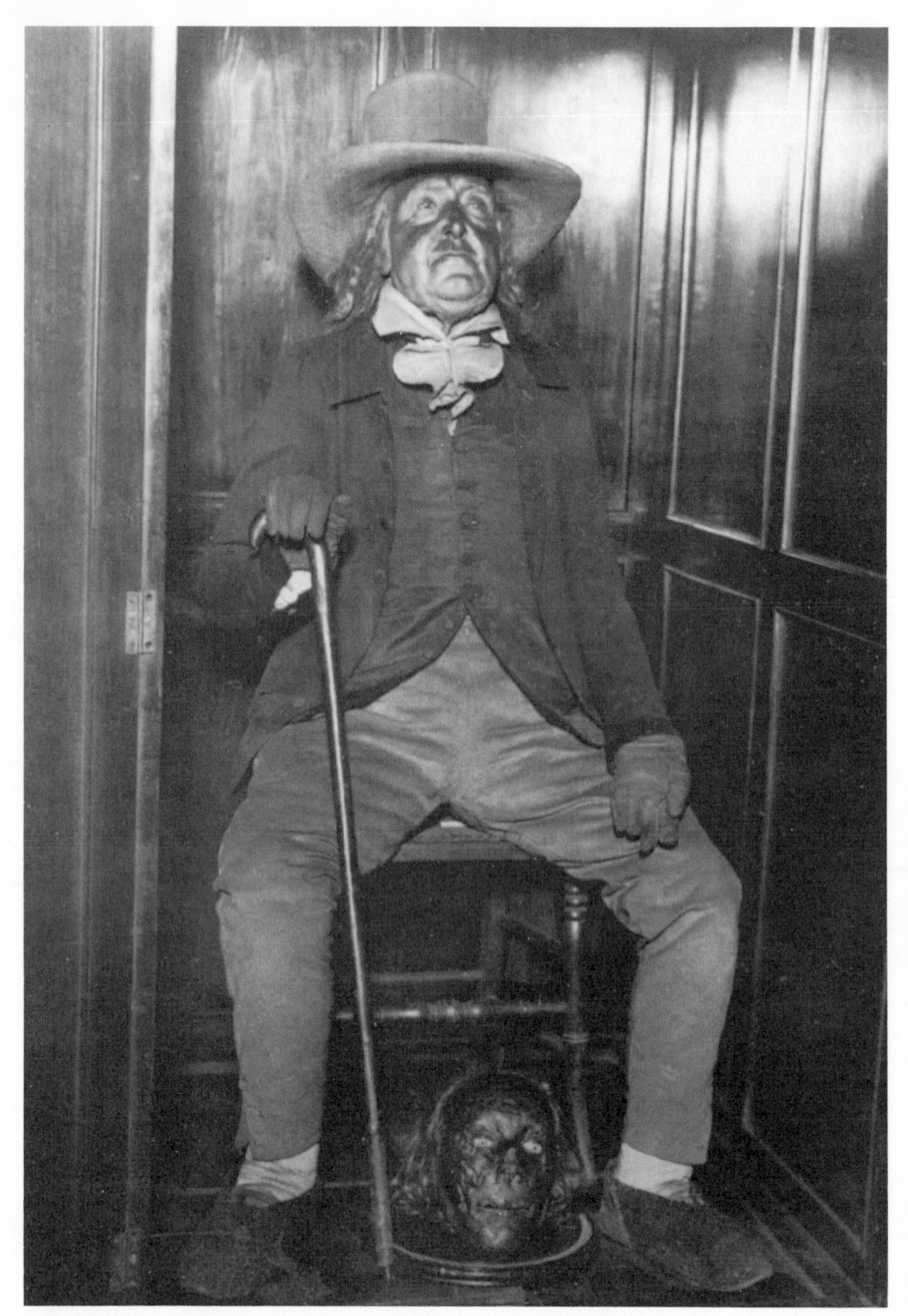

The stuffed body of Jeremy Bentham in University College, London

basis of morality was born in 1748. His name was Jeremy Bentham. One day, reading a pamphlet in an Oxford coffee house, he came across the phrase 'the greatest happiness of the greatest number'. On this phrase he built his whole system of law and morality.

Bentham believed in giving people as much freedom as possible, since, he argued, we ourselves usually know best what we want.

His strong belief in freedom meant that he didn't like governments interfering too much in citizens' lives. He believed, for instance, that the only reason for punishing anyone should be 'to exclude some greater evil'.

He once published two lists, a very short one setting out the duties of the government and a much longer one saying where governments should *not* interfere with their subjects' lives.

Bentham's major concern was to describe a society whose laws were designed to maximise happiness and minimise unhappiness. Anything in an action that promoted happiness Bentham called its usefulness or **utility**. Anything in an action that tended to promote unhappiness he called its **mischievousness**.

Utility and mischievousness

Utility, wrote Bentham, is 'that property in any object whereby it tends to produce pleasure, good or happiness, or to prevent the happening of mischief, pain, evil or unhappiness'.

According to Bentham, everyone has a duty to try to bring about the maximum happiness in the world. 'I learnt to see that *utility* was the test and measure of all virtue,' he said, 'and that the obligation to minister to general happiness was an obligation paramount to and inclusive of every other.' From this word 'utility', Bentham's theory of morals has become known as utilitarianism.

Utilitarianism

Morality, Bentham taught, requires us to act in a way that will produce the greatest happiness of the greatest number. And since everyone, young, old, clever or simple, desires pleasure and hates pain, Bentham's ideas demand that everyone be treated alike when it comes to working out ways of running society.

As he put it, 'Each to count as one, and none for more than one.' Unlike Epicurus, he refused to allow that some pleasures are finer than others. A popular game of the time was known as 'pushpin'. Bentham declared, 'Quantity of pleasure being equal, pushpin is as good as poetry.'

Bentham tried to make his principles as scientific as possible. He observed his fellow men and women and decided, as he put it, that 'Nature has placed mankind under the governance of two sovereign masters, *pain* and *pleasure*.' So he worked out four ways (or 'sanctions') for actually making men and women behave morally:

1 Society can force people to behave, by punishing them if they don't. This is Bentham's **physical** sanction.
2 Governments can pass laws, requiring people to behave, taking them to court if they don't. This is Bentham's **political** or **legal** sanction.
3 Our neighbours, and the opinions of our fellow countrymen can show disapproval of some actions and approval of others. This is Bentham's **social** sanction.
4 The churches can warn that God approves of some actions and disapproves of others. This is Bentham's **religious** sanction.

In consequence some people have described Bentham's views as the morality of the stick and the carrot. Basically it treats human beings the way people treat donkeys. If the donkey behaves badly, it gets the stick. If it behaves well, it gets a carrot.

Bentham became famous. The French made him an honorary citizen of their country. His ideas were put into practice throughout Europe and in America. When he died, according to his own will, his friends gathered together to see his body dissected. It was then put together again, with a wax head, dressed in his clothing, supplied with his walking-stick, and seated in a glass-fronted case in University College, London. There you can see him to this day.

Problems with utilitarianism

Yet although Bentham's teachings were welcomed by many, they still raise problems.

One problem with Bentham's utilitarianism is that you cannot add up different people's happiness the way you might add together say different people's money and so arrive at the total. In a school classroom, for instance, one pupil might be happiest at night clubs, another might be happiest playing chess, a third might be happiest playing hockey and a fourth might be happiest eating fish and chips. How can you add all these different pleasures together? It is really impossible to measure 'the greatest happiness of the greatest number'.

A second objection is that happiness is not necessarily a morally good thing. As Isaiah Berlin has written, 'If happiness is the sole criterion, then human sacrifice, or the burning of witches, at times when such practices had strong public feeling behind them, did doubtless, in their day, contribute to the happiness of the majority.' (Isaiah Berlin *Four Essays on Liberty*, OUP 1969, p192)

Thirdly, Bentham is not really talking about how to make people good, but simply of how to make them cunning enough to look after themselves in society. A prudent, sharp-sighted person who knows how to look after his or her own interests is not necessarily a virtuous one.

3 John Stuart Mill

One of Bentham's followers and friends, John Stuart Mill, was well aware of these objections and tried to deal with them.

Mill was especially concerned with Bentham's third 'sanction', the views of society. Suppose society's views were wrong. In that case society will tyrannise those it disagrees with, even if they are in the right. As Mill put it (in his *Essay on Liberty*, written in 1859), we need 'protection against the tyranny of the prevailing opinion and feeling; against the tendency of society to impose . . . its own ideas and practices as rules of conduct on those who dissent from them.'

The right to silence minority opposition

John Stuart Mill feared that the principle 'the greatest happiness of the greatest number' could lead to the majority silencing those whose views distressed them.

Mill knew that some of the greatest thinkers, such as the astronomer Galileo, had been silenced in their time by people in power whose views were simply wrong. He himself tirelessly campaigned for those groups in society who were unjustly treated in his own time: women, colonials, Southern American negroes, Irishmen. He had no faith that the views of the majority were always right.

'If all mankind were of one opinion, and one only person were of a contrary opinion,' Mill wrote, 'mankind would be no more justified in silencing that one person than he, if he had the power, would be justified in silencing mankind.'

Mill also found Bentham's view of happiness an extremely crude one. He asked whether or not some pleasures were preferable to others (just as we might ask whether, say, the pleasures of woodcarving are better than the pleasures of eating ice cream). Mere pleasure isn't everything. In Mill's own words, 'It is better to be Socrates dissatisfied than a fool satisfied.'

Conscience

As well as legal, penal, social and religious pressures to behave properly, set out by Jeremy Bentham, John Stuart Mill believed there was an even more powerful one inside all of us, namely conscience.

Mill described conscience as 'a feeling in our mind; a pain, more or less intense, attendant on violation of duty'.

When we do something which we really believe to be wrong, he said, we have to break through a mass of feeling, derived from our upbringing, our religion, our sympathy for others, fear of punishment, and the desire to be loved. This feeling Mill described as 'the essence of Conscience'.

Others had already identified this feeling. The Roman thinker Plutarch around the year AD 80 said that conscience was 'like an ulcer in the flesh, implanting in the soul a remorse after wrong-doing which never ceases to goad and wound it'.

St Paul on pagan conscience

St Paul believed that those who had never even come across the laws which God had given to the Jews, still could read the law in their own consciences. 'Pagans who never heard of the law but are led by reason to do what the law commands, may not actually "possess" the law, but they can be said to "be" the law,' he wrote. 'They can point to the substance of the law engraved on their hearts — they can call a witness, that is, their own conscience — they have accusation and defence, that is, their own inner mental dialogue.' (Romans chapter 2, verses 14f)

1 Weak consciences

Immanuel Kant believed God himself, in creating us, deliberately endows us with consciences. Nothing proved the greatness of God, he said, more than the starry heavens and the moral conscience within us. Not everyone has agreed with him. The pioneer psychologist Sigmund Freud (who didn't believe in God) sarcastically judged that if Kant was right about God's works, then 'although the stars are unquestionably superb, where conscience is concerned God has been guilty of an uneven and careless piece of work — for a great many people have only a limited share of it or scarcely enough to be worth mentioning.'

It is no doubt true that some people's consciences are weak, faulty and can easily be stifled. This does not mean that to follow our conscience is not a properly moral way of behaving.

2 Following your conscience

But a further point has often been made: to follow our conscience does not mean simply doing what we think fit. We also have brains. Before letting our conscience pass judgment on any proposed action, we need to find out all we can about what it involves. We need to ask who may suffer and who may benefit from our proposed action, before deciding what to do.

'Instructed' conscience

Christian teaching calls this following an 'instructed' conscience. An instructed conscience, said one of the greatest Catholic moral teachers (St Thomas Aquinas) must always be obeyed.

More help from religion

Our religious upbringing, as John Stuart Mill saw, helps to shape our conscience. All religions contain deep moral teachings, Christianity and Judaism especially insisting that God requires goodness from his people.

1 Charity

Old Testament view

The Jewish Bible makes it repeatedly clear that God's law demands charity towards the poor. 'Is there a poor man among you, one of your brothers, in any town of yours in the land that the Lord your God is giving you?' asks the book of Deuteronomy. 'Do not harden your heart or close your hand against that poor brother of yours, but be open-handed with him and lend him enough for his needs.' God, it is promised, will bless all those who help the poor with an open heart. 'Of course there will never cease to be poor in the land,' God says; 'I command you therefore: always be open-handed with your brother, and with anyone in your country who is in need and poor.' (Deuteronomy chapter 15, verses 7 to 11)

The Jewish prophets extended this teaching to include not only the poor but everyone in need. Isaiah cried:

> Let the oppressed go free,
> and break every yoke;
> share your bread with the hungry,
> and shelter the homeless poor;
> clothe the man you see naked,
> and do not turn away from your own kin.
> (Isaiah chapter 58, verse 7, JB)

The book of Job proclaims God's anger against those who grudge water to the thirsty man, refuse bread to the hungry, narrow the lands of the poor down to nothing, send widows away empty-handed and crush the arms of orphans. (Job chapter 22, verses 7 to 9)

2 Christian philanthropy

All this teaching was inherited by Christianity. Jesus once said, 'When you give a lunch or a dinner, do not ask your friends, brothers, relations or rich neighbours, for fear they repay your courtesy by inviting you in return. No, when you have a party, invite the poor, the crippled, the lame, the blind. That they cannot pay you back means that you are fortunate, for repayment will be made to you when the virtuous rise again.' (Luke chapter 14, verses 12 to 14)

Again, Jesus's disciple St James wrote: 'Pure, unspoilt religion, in the eyes of God our Father, is this: coming to the help of orphans and widows when they need it, and keeping oneself uncontaminated by the world.' (James chapter 1, verse 27) St James imagined a man welcoming two persons to worship God. One visitor was beautifully dressed with a gold ring on his finger. The other was dressed in shabby clothes. The rich man was taken to the best seats, and the poor man made to sit on the floor by his foot-rest. 'Can't you see that you have used two different standards in your mind,' said James, 'and turned yourselves into judges, and corrupt judges at that.' (James chapter 2, verses 2 to 4)

Double standards

This attack on double standards is found also in the Old Testament. It is a variant of Kant's law. You cannot have one rule for yourself and another rule for everyone else.

For instance, King David wanted another man's wife, a

woman named Bathsheba. He made love to her, and she became pregnant. At first David wanted to let people believe that the unborn child was the son of Bathsheba's husband. Then he thought of another way out. He told his army chief to put Bathsheba's husband in the thick of a battle, where he was certain to be killed.

This happened, and God's prophet Nathan heard about it. He decided to confront David, but in a brilliant way. He would make David condemn himself.

Nathan went to see the king and said:

> In the same town were two men, one rich, the other poor. The rich man had flocks and herds in great abundance: the poor man had nothing but a ewe lamb, one only, a small one he had bought. This he fed, and it grew up with him and his children, eating his bread, drinking from his own cup, sleeping on his breast; it was like a daughter to him.
>
> When there came a traveller to stay, the rich man refused to take one of his own flock or herd to provide for the wayfarer who had come to him. Instead he took the poor man's lamb and prepared it for his guest.

When David heard this story, he became angry at the injustice. 'As God lives,' he told Nathan, 'this man deserves to die.' David said that the rich man who had shown no compassion should be made to restore the poor man's lamb fourfold.

Nathan then revealed the meaning of his story, and said to King David, 'You are the man.' David was prepared to condemn another for stealing a man's sheep when he himself had stolen a man's wife. (2 Samuel chapter 11, verses 2 to 27, and chapter 12, verses 1 to 7, JB)

3 Later Christians

St Augustine on love

Other Christians built on the moral teachings of the Bible. St Augustine, who lived from the middle of the fourth century to AD 397, was one of the greatest. Following his master Jesus, Augustine taught that the greatest of all virtues was love. He then went on to say that love shows itself in four main ways:

1 in **justice**, producing a society whose goods are all used not selfishly but according to God's will;
2 in individual **self-control**, so that each man and woman remains pure and uncorrupted in the sight of God;

3 in **prudence**, a virtue because it stops us pursuing aims which will lead us astray and far from God's will for mankind;
4 in **strength of will**, so that whatever God demands of us, we do.

Of course Christians as well as others have often fallen far short of these aims. But the Christian ideal has never been lost, even at those times when many have been poor and starving while others were extremely rich — for instance in eighteenth-century England, when the poet William Blake was inspired to ask:

> Is this a holy thing to see
> In a rich a fruitful land
> Babes reduced to misery,
> Fed with cold and usurious hand?

The church speaks

Increasingly as the centuries passed, Christian bodies began to make statements about social life. Roman Catholic bishops come together in councils to work out their thoughts and pronounce on urgent questions. Between 1962 and 1965, for instance, they met frequently in Rome in the Vatican. Since there had been a Vatican Council in 1869–70, this second one is generally known as Vatican II.

Vatican II on needs of society

One important statement of Vatican II, issued in 1965, speaks of the role of Christians in today's world. 'There is a kind of person who boasts of grand and noble sentiments and lives in practice as if he could not care less about the needs of society,' wrote the bishops. 'Let everyone consider it his sacred duty to count social obligations among man's chief duties today and observe them as such.'

The statement goes on to discuss international aid. It argues:

> Christians should whole-heartedly support the establishment of an international order that includes genuine respect for legitimate freedom and friendly sentiments towards all men. This is all the more urgent now that the greater part of the world is in a state of such poverty. It is as if Christ himself were crying out in the

> mouths of these poor people to the charity of his disciples. Let us not be guilty of the scandal of having some nations, most of whose citizens bear the name of Christian, enjoying an abundance of riches while others lack the necessities of life and are tortured by hunger, disease and all kinds of misery.

The bishops added, 'We must praise and assist those Christians, especially those young Christians, who volunteer their services to help other men and other peoples.'

1 The popes

The leader of the world's Catholics, the pope, has also often felt the urgent need to advise Christians on difficult problems, usually in circular letters known as 'encyclicals'. At the end of the nineteenth century, for example, Pope Leo XIII sent out an encyclical attacking the way working men and women were so frequently treated abominably by their employers. His encyclical defended the workers' right to join together in trade unions and professional associations.

'Peace on Earth' encyclical

In 1963 Pope John XXIII sent out a powerful encyclical called 'Peace on Earth'. In it he set out how a Christian should understand the rights of all human beings. Everyone, declared the Pope, had the right to:

1 those earthly goods necessary for a decent life;
2 freedom of enquiry, in religious as in other matters, so that men and women may decide for themselves what to believe;
3 conditions of work acceptable to human dignity;
4 the ability to worship God according to one's own conscience.

The Pope also wrote about social justice between nations. 'As everybody knows,' he said, 'there are countries with an abundance of arable land and a scarcity of man-power, while in other countries there is no proportion between natural resources and the capital available. This demands that peoples should set up relationships of mutual collaboration, making easy the circulation from one country to another of capital, goods and man-power.'

2 Individual Christian leaders

Individual Christians sometimes achieve a stature in the

Archbishop Desmond Tutu condemning apartheid

world that gives what they have to say great importance. One example is the Anglican Archbishop of Johannesburg, Desmond Tutu.

Desmond Tutu on apartheid

When the South African government suspected that the South African Council of Churches was promoting the cause of black men and women in a way contrary to official white policy, it summoned the Council's general secretary, Desmond Tutu, to an inquiry.

The South African Council of Churches has 12 million members. Desmond Tutu was its first black general secretary. For his opposition to apartheid he won the Nobel Peace Prize.

He took the opportunity of the inquiry to make a clear statement of his views on religion and the rights of all human beings. 'When God encounters injustice, oppression, exploitation, he takes sides. Then God and the Bible are subversive of such a situation,' he declared.

Desmond Tutu added: 'I want the Government to know now and always that I do not fear them. They are trying to defend the indefensible. Apartheid is as evil and vicious as Nazism and Communism, and the Government will fail completely, for it is ranging itself on the side of evil, injustice and oppression.'

Dom Helder Câmara

Dom Helder Câmara was consecrated Roman Catholic archbishop of poverty-stricken Olinde and Recife, Brazil, in 1964.

When he was assistant Roman Catholic bishop of Rio de Janeiro, Helder Câmara saw at first hand the wretchedness of those who live in the shanty towns on the outskirts of that city. He began to preach from his pulpit and on television that the church must take a lead in distributing its wealth to the poor.

The Brazilian authorities began to harass the archbishop. His home was attacked with machine guns. Helder Câmara continued to take the side of the poor, attacking those who, he considered, sought only their own profit at the expense of the rest of Brazilian society.

Conscious of the attacks often made by the powerful on those who try to live according to God's will, Archbishop Helder Câmara has written, 'If the Church is to give the example it must, if it is to be the living presence of Christ among men and with men, it urgently and permanently needs to cast off its concern for prestige, to unharness itself from the chariot of the mighty, and to agree to live the prophecy of the Master, which is valid for all times: "Behold, I send you out as sheep in the midst of wolves . . . They will hand you over to courts of judgment."' (Matthew chapter 10, verses 16f)

Helder Câmara continues:

> This is the difficult and radiant poverty that God asks of his Son's Church today: to sever all compromises with governments and the powerful, and to commit itself to the service of the poor, the oppressed, the destitute, the sons of God who are made to live subhuman lives.
>
> (Cardinal Suenens and Dom Helder Câmara *Charismatic Renewal and Social Action: A Dialogue*, Darton Longman and Todd 1980, p55)

Yet Helder Câmara still hopes that all men may see the light of God's teachings. He therefore prays not just for the poor but for the rich. He calls the rich 'our brothers', believing that God can forgive all men if they will turn to him. This is Helder Câmara's prayer for the rich.

A prayer for the rich

> Lord, you alone hold
> life, knowledge, freedom.

A shanty town in Brazil.

You alone
possess the true wealth
which cannot be devalued
and remains beyond the grave,
the wealth men share
without becoming poorer.

Grant that our brothers, the rich
may understand that gold
has no money-power in the Beyond;
that in the land of eternity
love alone is accepted
as authentic currency.

Grant that their too-favoured children
may discover the plight of the poor
and not shirk their social duty.
May they not be corrupted by ease
but learn the value of sacrifice
so that a better world may dawn
not against but for them.'

(ibid., p81)

3 The World Council of Churches

Just as Roman Catholic leaders regularly meet to apply the teachings of Christianity to today's world, so members of the many other churches in the world have set up their own international body, the World Council of Churches. This body was created in 1948 by representatives of 147 churches coming from 44 countries.

In 1961, when the World Council of Churches was holding a general assembly at New Delhi, India, the churches of the East (known as 'Orthodox' churches and including the important Russian Orthodox church) joined.

A later general assembly, held at Uppsala, declared that Christians are called by Jesus not just to pray and worship but also to work 'in the struggle for economic justice against the exploitation of people by people . . . in the struggle for human dignity against political oppression of human beings by their fellow men . . . in the struggle of hope against despair in personal life.'

Churches' message from Uppsala

The message of Uppsala included these words.

We heard the cry of those who long for peace; of the

hungry and exploited who demand bread and justice; of the victims of discrimination who claim human dignity; and of the increasing millions who seek for the meaning of life. God hears these cries and judges us.

Learning from other religions

Although, as the World Council of Churches puts it, Christians are those who believe in Jesus 'as God and Saviour according to the Scriptures', this does not mean that we cannot learn from the deep moral teachings found in the other great religions of the world.

This book has already drawn on Jewish as well as Christian teachings. Three other important world religions are Buddhism, Islam and Hinduism.

1 Buddhist ethics

Buddhism is a religion preaching above all compassion and mercy.

The Buddha told his followers not to waste their time or their money on extravagance or selfish pleasures. All Buddhists are obliged to obey four rules:

Four rules

1 not to take what is not given;
2 not to lie;
3 not to indulge in unlawful sexual intercourse;
4 not to kill.

Some Buddhists also teach a fifth rule: not to drink alcohol.

2 The Qur'an

Islam, the religion of Muslims, is based essentially on the teachings of the Qur'an — revelations made to the prophet Muhammad between the years 610 and 632 after the birth of Jesus. They were written down some time after his death, and are regarded by Muslims as the word of God.

The Qur'an teaches that a wrong done to anyone else is 'a wrong done against oneself'. Greed, fraud and a refusal to spend on the poor are condemned by God. The rich are to be taxed to help the poor. Orphans and widows must be cared for. Although men may marry up to four wives, if a man fears he cannot treat several wives with equal justice, he must marry only one. And as the Qur'an puts it, the noblest persons in the sight of God are the ones who are most righteous.

3 A Hindu holy book and its influence on Gandhi

The *Bhagavadgita* is the holiest book of the Hindu religion. Amongst those who have been profoundly influenced by it was Gandhi (see pages 99–104, 105).

Mahatma Gandhi called the *Bhagavadgita* his 'spiritual dictionary'. He learned above all two things from it:

Samabhava

1 the spirit of *samabhava*, a Sanskrit word meaning 'equability'. An equable person, according to the *Bhagavadgita*, remains totally unaffected and undisturbed by what happens to him or her. Striving for good may not succeed. Pleasure may turn to pain. Victory may turn into defeat. The equable man or woman fears none of this, but continues his or her life-task in peace of mind.

Aparigraph

2 the spirit of *aparigraph*, a Sanskrit word which means 'non-possession'. On this the *Bhagavadgita* taught Gandhi to cease to care for lands, money or property. Material goods, it taught, can squeeze the spirit dry.

   This spirit enabled Gandhi to become closer in touch with the lives of India's poor. He promoted simple cottage industries, spinning by hand and weaving his own clothing.

The supreme command

Nearly all great religions base themselves to some extent on sacred writings, which we call scriptures. And then they find in these scriptures specially important passages which express the essentials of their teachings.

For St Paul, the gift of loving others with no desire to satisfy yourself is the greatest virtue of a Christian. He put it higher than faith itself, higher than knowledge, higher than hope. He wrote:

If I have all the eloquence of men or of angels, but speak

without love, I am simply a gong booming or a cymbal clashing. If I have the gift of prophecy, understanding all the mysteries there are, and knowing everything, and if I have faith in all its fullness, to move mountains, but without love, then I am nothing at all. If I give away all that I possess piece by piece, and if I even let them take my body to burn it, but am without love, it will do me no good whatever.

Love is always patient and kind; it is never jealous; love is never boastful or conceited; it is never rude or selfish; it does not take offence, and is not resentful. Love takes no pleasure in other people's sins but delights in the truth; it is always ready to excuse, to trust, to hope, and to endure whatever comes.

Love does not come to an end. But if there are gifts of prophecy, the time will come when they must fail; or the gift of languages, it will not continue for ever; and knowledge — for this, too, the time will come when it must fail . . .

In short, there are three things that last: faith, hope and love; and the greatest of these is love.'

(1 Corinthians chapter 13, verses 1 to 8 and 13, JB)

Questions and coursework

1 How many commandments which the Jews received from Moses do Christians regard as specially important?
2 Write down three of Moses's commandments.
3 We all often must decide the difference between right and ....
4 Jesus said, 'Happy are the ....; they shall have mercy shown to them.'
5 Moral behaviour based on what makes you happiest is called ....
6 'Pleasure is the be-all and end-all of life,' wrote a Greek called ....
7 Who based his morality on the phrase 'the greatest happiness of the greatest number'?
8 Amongst the pressures which help to make us behave properly is a powerful feeling inside us which we call ....

9 St Augustine taught that the greatest of all virtues is ....

10 In 1948, 147 Christian churches from many countries in the world set up a body known as the ....

11 Name three holy books from the religions of the world.

12 'There are three things that last,' wrote St Paul: 'faith, hope and love; and the greatest of these is ....'

13 What do you understand to be the meaning of 'Love your neighbour as yourself'?

14 What do you understand 'hedonism' to be?

15 Define an 'egoist'.

16 Do you think that conscience alone can be a sufficient guide to knowing how you should behave?

17 What is your understanding of utilitarianism?

18 Is pursuing happiness a morally good thing?

19 It is often said, 'You mustn't go against your conscience.' What does this mean? Give an example (true or invented) of someone who went against his or her conscience.

20 Using your own research, write an account of the World Council of Churches.

21 What moral teachings can we learn from Buddhism, Islam and Hinduism?

22 Some people argue that wealthier countries like Britain and the USA should give much more money and help to Third World countries. Others argue that if countries are poor it is their own fault — they are not our responsibility. Which point of view do you share? Give reasons.

23 Read the following passage and answer all the questions a to g.

> In a famous novel, called *Crime and Punishment*, the main character plots and carries out the murder of an old woman who has a considerable amount of money in her apartment. After killing her, he steals the money.

He argues that:

> (1) she is a spiteful, argumentative and scheming old woman, useless to herself and to society, and her life causes no happiness to herself or to others;

and

> (2) her money, if found after her death, would only fall into the hands of cheats, whereas he would use it for his education.

(a) Which word in argument 1 above suggests utilitarianism?
(b) What is there in argument 2 above which suggests that the man might be arguing like a utilitarian?
(c) Why might some utilitarians refuse to make rules like 'Do not kill'?
(d) What is said about murder in the Sermon on the Mount when Jesus contrasts his teaching with the Law?
(e) In what way does Jesus go further than this, when he describes attitudes towards enemies?
(f) Using New Testament material, suggest what is distinctive about the motives and attitudes required of Christians.
(g) Should a Christian oppose the action and motives of the man in the novel? Give reasons for your answer.

24 What do you know about Dom Helder Câmara?
25 What do you know about Martin Luther King?

Some Books

John Balchin *What Christians Believe*, Lion 1984

*P Baelz *Ethics and Belief*, Sheldon Press 1977

James Bentley *Martin Niemöller*, Hodder and Stoughton 1986

James and Audrey Bentley *The Life and Teaching of Jesus*, Longman 1986

James and Audrey Bentley *Christianity*, Longman 1987

I Birnie *Christians and Social Work*, Arnold 1969

Helder Câmara *The Desert is Fertile*, Sheed and Ward 1974

M A Chignell *Perspectives*, Arnold 1981

D P Church and B G Ford *Focus on World Problems*, Nelson, 2nd edition 1975

Steve Elsworth *Acid Rain*, Pluto Press 1985

David Field *Christianity in the Modern World*, Hulton 1983

David Field and Peter Toon *Real Questions*, Lion 1982

Tom Gardiner *Thinking for Life*, Arnold 1984

Bob Geldof *Is That It?*, Penguin Books 1986

*Maurice Ginsberg *On Justice in Society*, Penguin Books 1965

F G Herod *Who Cares?*, Methuen 1981

*Ted Honderich *Punishment. The Supposed Justifications*, Hutchinson 1969

C S King *My Life with Martin Luther King*, Hodder and Stoughton 1970

Martin Luther King *Strength to Love*, SCM Press 1964

*Richard Lindley, Roger Fellows and Graham Macdonald *What Philosophy Does*, Open Books 1978

Mike Nicholson *Mahatma Gandhi*, Exley Publications 1987

*Reinhold Niebuhr *Christian Realism and Political Problems*, Charles Scribner's 1952

*P H Nowell-Smith *Ethics*, Penguin Books 1954

R J Owen *Christian Aid*, Religious and Moral Education Press 1983

M Pennock *Moral Problems*, Ave Maria Press 1980

M Pennock and J Finley *Christian Morality and You*, Ave Maria Press 1976

*John Rawls *A Theory of Justice*, OUP 1972

David Sheppard *Bias to the Poor*, Hodder and Stoughton 1983

John Stott *Issues Facing Christians Today*, Marshall Morgan and Scott 1984

Cardinal Suenens and Dom Helder Câmara *Charismatic Renewal and Social Action*, Darton Longman and Todd 1980

E J Taylor *Problems of Christian Living*, Blackie 1978

*Helmut Thielicke *Theological Ethics*, Vol. II, *Politics*, A & C Black 1969

B Wakeman *Personal, Social and Moral Education*, Lion 1984

Anne Wilkinson *It's not fair*, Christian Aid 1985

Gibson Winter (editor) *Social Ethics*, SCM Press 1968

Books marked with an asterisk (*) will probably be unsuitable for all but the advanced students.

Index

Acknowledgements

We are grateful to the following for permission to reproduce copyright material:

Darton, Longman and Todd Ltd & Servant Publications for extracts from *Charismatic Renewal and Social Action* by Cardinal Suenens & Dom Helder Camara, published and copyright by Darton, Longman and Todd & Servant Publications 1980; Guardian Newspapers Ltd for the article 'Iranian Halts Jet in Asylum Protest' from *The Guardian* 10 September 1987; Michael R. Hughes for his letter in *The Times* 3 September 1987; Times Newspapers Ltd for extracts from articles in *The Times* 4 September 1987 and *The Sunday Times* 30 August 1987, (c) Times Newspapers Ltd 1987.

We are grateful to the following for permission to reproduce photographs:

BBC Hulton Picture Library, pages 101, 105 (photo: Bettmann Newsphotos), 148, Department of Health and Social Security, page 133; The Family Planning Association, page 122; Sally & Richard Greenhill, pages 14, 118, 129; Greenpeace Communications, page 38 (photo: Vennemann); Paul Hamann, page 79; John & Penny Hubley, page 47 below; International Defence & Aid Fund for Southern Africa, pages 11, 158; The Keystone Collection, page 92; Network, pages 70 (photo: Katalin Arkell), 72 (photo: Denis Doran), 97 (photo: Steve Benbow), 110 (photo: Barry Lewis); Oxfam, pages 47 above (photo: Nick Fogden), 160 (photo: C Pearson); Press Association, page 75; Carlos Reyes, page 30; Rex Features, page 144; Syndication International (1986) Ltd, page 52; Universal Pictorial Press, page 22; Voluntary Service Overseas, page 54 (photo: Rob Short); The Wiener Library, London, page 7.

Abbreviations in text:
JB Jerusalem Bible, published by Darton, Longman and Todd, 1966
RSV Revised Standard Version of the Bible, Copyrighted 1971 and 1952 by the Division of Christian Education of the National Council of the Churches of Christ in the USA. Published by Thomas Nelson & Sons Ltd, 1946 & 1952
NEB New English Bible, published by Oxford University Press and Cambridge University Press
Other Bible quotations are the authors' versions.

By the same authors

The Life and Teaching of Jesus

- Concise but thorough treatment with close reference to GCSE requirements
- Clear and well-structured, beginning with a brief introduction and background to the gospels, followed by a detailed and thought-provoking study of the life and teaching of Jesus
- Readable and well-documented, encouraging a better understanding of Jesus and his teaching
- Variety of questions for classwork, discussion, ideas for further work or for coursework.

- Concise but thorough treatment with close reference to GCSE requirements
- A thought-provoking study of the themes and aspects of Christianity over the centuries and today
- Examines and explains in detail the major Catholic, Protestant, Orthodox and Anglican traditions
- Encourages pupils to assess the importance of Christianity today and to express their own views on Christian teaching, morality and practice
- Varied suggestions of coursework, guided by the GCSE national criteria, accompany each chapter
- Students are encouraged to show what they *know*, what they *understand* and how they can evaluate the material